Dictionary of Country Furniture

MARJORIE FILBEE

Dictionary of Country Furniture

HEARST BOOKS

NEW YORK

First published 1977
by The Connoisseur
Chestergate House
Vauxhall Bridge Road
London SW1V 1HF

ISBN 0-90030-517-7

Drawings by Patrick Filbee
Cover picture by Oliver and Sheila Mathews
Designed by Derek Morrison
Edited by Isabel Sutherland
Consultant Editor, David Coombs

The publishers wish to thank the many museums and other organizations which have co-operated in supplying photographs for this book; Mr and Mrs Elton Jones for their kind permission to allow us to photograph the room shown on the front cover; and the Curator of the Castle Museum, York, for permission to use the photograph of the Moorland Cottage of 1850 on the back cover. The source for the drawings, where known, is indicated in the accompanying text although in some instances, to our regret, we have been unable to discover the present owner.

Filmset and printed in Great Britain by
BAS Printers Limited, Over Wallop, Hampshire
and bound by
Cambridge University Press, Cambridge

To my husband

Acknowledgments

I am very grateful to those writers whose work has shown an interest in country furniture, and also wish to thank my local library at Lymington for their help in obtaining copies of the older books. I am particularly grateful to the staff and curators of various museums for help in tracking down the country pieces in their possession, especially Patricia Butler at Ipswich Museum, and Ivan Sparkes at the High Wycombe Chair Museum who was so generous in allowing me to use material from his two books *The English Country Chair* and *The Windsor Chair*. I would also like to thank the staff and curators of The American Museum in Britain, The Museum of English Rural Life, the National Museum of Antiquities of Scotland, the Welsh Folk Museum at St Fagans, the Highland Folk Museum, Kingussie, and Anthony Wells-Cole at Temple Newsam House, Leeds, pioneers in modern furniture research into local styles; also the Victoria and Albert Museum, London. Thanks are due also to the publishers of *Welsh Furniture*, by L. Twiston-Davies and H. J. Lloyd-Johnes, for permission to quote from this book; all the drawings of Welsh furniture were based on photographs taken from this work. Finally I would like to thank Victor Chinnery for his help over caquetoire chairs and for the information as to the group of Salisbury chairs. My special thanks go to Edward Joy for patiently reading the manuscript, and to Patrick Filbee for the drawings.

Marjorie Filbee

Contents

Introduction

Many words have been written on all aspects of the fashionable furniture found in town houses and our statelier homes in the countryside during the last three hundred years. The study of the furniture of smaller country homes, farmhouses and cottages during this period has been sadly neglected, and it is only comparatively recently that this truly vernacular furniture, from the homes of what was the greater mass of the people until the 19th century, has been considered worthy of attention. Writing in 1912, Arthur Hayden, one of the earliest pioneers on the subject, pleaded for special research on local furniture before it was dispersed far and wide and its identity with particular districts lost for ever. It was to be another fifty years before much modern research was turned in this direction, apart from the work of a mere handful of writers.

The furniture included in this book is the furniture that has graced these smaller country homes, most of it dating from the 17th, 18th and 19th centuries, made by local craftsmen from the wood of the trees that grew near to hand. Much of it is still in the homes it has furnished for many years and no doubt a great deal of it is still in the same position in those homes, because so many pieces were made for a particular corner that no newer piece would fit so well; but examples of much of the furniture described can be found in many museums and houses open to the public in various parts of Britain. Some of these are listed in the section at the end of this book.

The author's aim has been both to help owners or prospective purchasers of country furniture to identify various pieces and styles and to give some idea of their history. This history is the story of what has been called 'the unhurried heart of England'. It is the history of ordinary people who went their way surprisingly uninfluenced by changes in kings and queens, governments or imported fashions, living much the same lives in 1750 as they did in 1650 or 1850. Their furniture was handmade by village craftsmen, in many cases the village carpenter who had time to make furniture only when not engaged in more important work, building the timber frames and fittings of farmhouses, farm buildings and making farm implements. Even country joiners spent a great deal of their time making doors and general house fittings as well as furniture.

This being so, a few basic principles guided the work of rural craftsmen and influenced all the country furniture we are considering. The furniture was generally made to specific orders; only in the larger country workshops was enough furniture made to have a selection in hand from which a customer could choose. 'Please make me a table', would be the request. Unless the customer had any ideas of his own, the craftsman was free to make it to his own design, usually based on one which had been handed down from generation to generation.

Some basic principles

The most important necessity was durability. The craftsman certainly didn't want his customer coming back in the foreseeable future to tell him his work was falling apart and needed repair. Life was too short. He was far removed from the disposable or throwaway age, so country furniture was first and foremost solidly constructed, from solid wood using well-tried methods. Perhaps this is one of the reasons we are so attracted to it today.

The second principle that guided the craftsman was to make a piece of furniture fit for the life and purpose for which it was needed. A cupboard would have to fit a particular corner or alcove, or accommodate a low sloping ceiling; drawers would be placed in a particular part of a dresser and be of a certain size for good reasons and particular needs, so there is a variety in country pieces never found in the mass-produced kind. Stools were usually three legged and often chairs as well, as the safest means of coping with balancing on uneven farmhouse floors. Chair legs were joined by stretchers long after these horizontal members had gone out of fashion on town chairs, again for stability and sturdiness but also because floors were draughty and often dirty and feet needed to be kept off floors by resting them on a stretcher. Settles had high backs to make a draught-free corner round a fireplace at the end of a hard day in the open air. If country seating often seems hard and unyielding, shelter and warmth were probably more important than comfort, and cushions were no doubt always used. The countryman's life, in any case, didn't allow much time for lounging.

The third principle that influenced country furniture was that the country craftsman used wood that was near to hand, so that he was able to select the pieces that were the most suitable for whatever he was constructing. He would take special care in choosing a piece of wood that he knew would be subject to extra stress, just as a wheelwright would need to choose his wood with great care to make a waggon that would withstand the strain. In fact the wheelwright was often the village carpenter and furniture maker as well. Only when furniture is made by hand rather than mass produced can this careful selection of suitable wood be made.

While much of the furniture that is still with us was made of oak, a great deal must have been made in other less durable woods, such as the great variety of fruitwoods, which have long since perished; but there are still some fine pieces of country furniture in elm and yew to be seen, several of which appear among the illustrations.

Besides durability, and apart from constructional details such as the fact that oak was easy to split with a wedge before saws were used, another important reason for the use of so much oak was that its surface stood up to hard wear, and the dents and knocks of everyday life don't appear to distract from its beauty, as in the case of the highly polished and smoother surfaces of walnut and mahogany. The attraction is in the grain and colour of the wood itself and the patina acquired through many years of wear and polishing. This is an effect difficult to acquire in reproduction pieces, a point to be remembered by intending purchasers.

Guidelines for the collector
This patination, in fact, is of more importance than signs of wear, which are really not so disastrous in furniture for country homes, but which add to the character of each piece, helping it to fit into an old house, where a brand new piece of furniture might look out of place. Worn stretchers where feet have rested, worn sides where hands and feet have rocked cradles for generations, show that the furniture has been part of the lives of the people using it. They have left their impression on it in a way that it is impossible to do on articles of man-made materials. This gives a feeling of continuity, serenity and timelessness that makes the furniture fit into a modern country home without difficulty. Country furniture made by modern craftsmen by traditional methods in solid wood will soon acquire this character as it settles into the lives of its new owners.

It is more important to concentrate on the appearance of the wood and the craftsmanship of the construction when buying a piece of country furniture, rather than on the date it was made or who made it, facts which influence the purchase of so much town furniture. Because styles persisted for so long in rural areas, because the names of very few makers are known, and because, apart from inventories and probate records, there is little documentation of country furniture, dating a particular piece is difficult. Poor workmanship does not necessarily mean that the piece of furniture is older. In towns a new piece of furniture was not likely to have been purchased in an old-fashioned style, but this does not apply to our country pieces. Catalogues of furniture makers in towns indicate dates, but are few outside towns.

The inventories highlight another difficulty in sorting out the various styles and putting a name to them. We know that one term has different meanings in different parts of the country, and at different dates. Dower chests are sometimes referred to as linen chests or blanket chests. Arks were also known as hutches, a word that has also covered large flour chests, food cupboards, small chests and has ended up today as a home for rabbits. Coffer is another word used for anything from a small leather-covered travelling chest, a flour chest, or a Bible box.

Some of the words used in the modern world of antiques are also unhelpful. It seems to be obsessed with monasteries, describing pieces as 'refectory tables' and 'monk's benches' when these items are more likely to have been associated with the village inn at the time they were made. The terms used now were not contemporary. However, if the terms in the inventories are ambiguous, the descriptive adjectives used in some 18th century Essex inventories give no doubt as to the state of some of the furniture in them, such as 'one indeferant bed' or 'two sorry old chaires'.

American furniture

Probably the Americans have always used more direct names than the British for their furniture; armchairs being distinguished from single chairs by being called 'great' chairs; butterfly tables, tallboys and lowboys giving some picture of the articles to which they applied before further description is added. American furniture is better documented than that of the United Kingdom and therefore easier to date; the Americans appear always to have been interested in the history of their early country furniture.

American furniture is also easier to sort out into various styles in use in the 17th and 18th centuries, which assists the study of early furniture this side of the Atlantic. This is due to the fact that the early colonists who left England for America remained in fairly isolated groups for some time, and had more contact with the country they had left behind than with each other, so the styles of the district they came from were most prominent in their furniture during the early years of colonization.

This in turn also helps us to study something of the early furniture of the various nationalities that eventually settled in America, such as the Germans, Dutch, Swiss, French and Spanish. We find many similarities that are fascinating and can also see how styles from Europe soon developed along distinctive American lines. A good example of this can be seen in the study of American Windsor chairs (see A–Z section).

Influences on the English craftsmen

Styles in England were dispersed more quickly due to the greater mobility of the population, making it difficult to say that a certain design came from one particular area, but research being done on both sides of the Atlantic is helping to make the picture clearer. This is seen particularly in connection with the study of designs on chests and chairbacks of the 17th century, before travel gradually became easier and before the pattern books of 18th century designers spread designs all over the country. Interesting areas of furniture design and ornamentation are being discovered in small pockets of craftsmanship all over England.

The population of England has always been fairly mobile from an early date, especially the wealthier classes, so it has always been possible for craftsmen in rural areas to see new designs and incorporate them in their work, if they wished to do so. Inventories of a Devonshire village from 1576–1769 show the conservatism of village tastes. During two hundred years the furniture remained consistent, but the inventories show that the villagers were not slow to adopt new ideas for which they could find a use. Clocks and tea sets, for example, appear in the village soon after they were in general use in towns. If a new style was rejected by a countryman it was not, as a townsman might think, for the reason that he had never heard of it, but because it did not fit into his way of life or that he did not see any good reason to change.

In the small communities of earlier times the country craftsman was seldom far from the castle owner, lord of the manor or squire. He could hardly fail to notice their homes and the contents of them, especially when they were forever moving their belongings in public from one place to another. The great cathedrals built over several hundred years, embodying all the changes in art, craftsmanship and architecture of the ages in which they were built, were designed to instruct and inform those who worshipped there, as was every parish church. They hadn't the austere interiors we admire today. The walls, windows and stonework would have been a riot of colour, pictures and patterns and the woodwork painted to make the most impression on those who gazed on them. It was meant to be a vision of heaven on earth, as well as the vivid pictures of hell painted on their walls.

It is inconceivable that even a village carpenter in the Middle Ages, who was responsible for all the woodwork and furniture in his village, wouldn't have been influenced by what he saw around him. The Gothic patterns and tracery of early furniture are proof of what a strong influence the church was. As the churches were bright, so were the homes. The houses were not as dark and dismal as we might imagine from antique oak furniture remaining. The oak was originally light in colour and has only become dark with age. We know that like church woodwork it was sometimes painted; traces of this still survive. Tapestries and carpets were used for coverings for furniture and walls, which were also painted.

All the furniture and furnishings of medieval homes were movable. Considering the state of the roads, medieval times were famous for their travellers. The king as well as castle and manor owners appear to have been in a state of perpetual motion from one of their homes to another, together with their retainers, and joined by an assorted crowd of pilgrims along the way. While modern caravan owners take their home and the kitchen stove with them, medieval travellers took the wall coverings and even window glass, in the days when this was scarce and costly. In those unsettled times it was safer to take everything with you than leave it at home. Possessions were simple and very few when times were dangerous, and any spare money was spent on quickly moved materials to decorate walls and furniture, rather than on the furniture itself.

Gradual change

It is difficult for us to imagine how slowly things altered during the many centuries before the industrial revolution and the last two hundred years of scientific progress. Many articles such as chests and stools have been in use from the beginning of our history. Others, such as chairs, became increasingly popular only after home life became more peaceful and prosperous in the reign of Elizabeth I, when furniture became more plentiful and permanent, and greater care was lavished on its making. Only gradually did buildings become homes and not merely fortified houses with communal living.

It was a slow process; chimneys and fireplaces became more common and the building of extra rooms for the sake of privacy resulted in the development of more articles of furniture for their various uses, and the storage of increased possessions. Farm and cottage produced their own food and made most of their own clothing, furniture and farm implements apart from those made by village craftsmen. Scarcity of furniture was due to lack of space as well as lack of money. In many of the much photographed weavers' cottages in East Anglia one has to remember that the most important article in them was the weaving loom, not a small article to house in so small a space. Early industry was more often than not carried on in the home.

It is important to realise the improvement in the position of yeoman farmers during the 16th and 17th centuries. Changes took place in the countryside from the end of the 14th century onwards, when the feudal system in England had broken down. This was partly due to the lack of labour for the land after the plagues of the 14th century, when there was a change from arable to sheep farming, with a resulting increase in the prosperity of the farmers concerned in it, over the next two centuries. Many of the beautiful farmhouses of our countryside were built and furnished during this period. The joiners took over most of the furniture making with panel and frame construction, making chests, cupboards and tables lighter than they had ever been before. The joiners' construction of the 16th and 17th centuries became standard construction for most country furniture until the 20th century.

The craftsmen's functions

While the Guilds for the control of the standard of workmanship of the various craftsmen grew during these early centuries, they had little control over country workers. Demarcation disputes between workers are no new thing and many took place as to the functions of carpenters, joiners and turners until the various crafts became separated in the 17th century. Again this did not apply so much in country areas where often one craftsman in a village fulfilled several functions. Chairmaking became a separate craft in the 17th century and the work of locksmiths and blacksmiths also became separate crafts leading to the gradual evolution of more delicate work for furniture fittings in various metals.

The 17th century saw not only the separation of woodworkers into different classes but the rise of a new craftsman, the cabinet maker who worked in new imported woods such as walnut and mahogany, using veneers and new methods of construction which completely changed the styles of furniture that could be produced. No longer was it possible to see at a glance how a piece of furniture was made, as one could when looking at a piece made by a carpenter and a joiner.

The great dividing line between town and country furniture came in 1660 with the restoration of Charles II to the throne. The violent reaction against the Puritan styles of the Commonwealth period resulted in the opening of the country to an influx of foreign craftsmen. These brought both the methods of construction and flamboyant styles of the furniture made by cabinet makers that the king and his followers had come to know while in exile in France and the Low Countries. The introduction of new furniture styles in London was accelerated by the Great Fire of London in 1666, which destroyed so many homes and the furniture in them, resulting in the rebuilding and refurnishing in new styles on a large scale.

The work of the cabinet makers in London and the larger towns became more and more specialized, until in the 18th century the making of fashionable furniture started on the drawing board designed by men whose names are now household words, but who in most cases produced little of the finished products themselves.

The yeoman farmers

In the countryside there was comparatively little change. When the landed gentry lost the Civil War much valuable furniture and plate passed into the hands of the yeoman farmers who had remained neutral during the war years, quietly amassing fortunes, which their descendants enjoyed until the 19th century. Farmhouses have always acquired furniture from the wealthier homes when it needed to be replaced by newer fashions and no doubt many styles were gradually copied and adapted from furniture acquired in this way. The pattern books of the 18th century designers circulated all over the country and the country craftsman produced simplified and individual versions, later in date, of these designs, in oak and local woods to satisfy his customers who had seen the new styles in town. For the most part he continued to produce his traditional furniture constructed in the same way it had been since the 16th century.

The yeoman farmers of the 17th and 18th century were quite high up the social scale of the time, meeting and marrying with the families of the squire, the doctor, the parson, the attorney and the merchant. Only with the coming of the industrial revolution were there again changes in the countryside.

Fashion and tradition

In Victorian times mass-produced furniture became widespread and country furniture began to lose much of its character and reflected the fashions of the town more than it had ever done in the past, but it was only in the late 19th century that much factory-made furniture began to find its way into country farmhouses. However, by the time William Cobbett made his rural rides in 1825 he was complaining that in a farm he had visited the good plain furniture of former years had been neglected and an attempt made to follow town fashions. There was even a parlour where there was 'the mahogany table and the fine chairs and the fine glass, and all as bare-faced upstart as any stock-jobber in the kingdom can boast of'.

In spite of this, from 1700 in the Buckinghamshire area of HighWycombe the country craftsmen produced their most famous item of country furniture, the Windsor chair, embodying all that was best in traditional craftsmanship. The chair has been made continuously since then and is still produced there today by firms founded by some of the earliest names in the High Wycombe chair industry. Always a joint product of several craftsmen, the Windsor chair made a smooth transition to factory methods when the time came.

But even in Victorian times not all country furniture was despised and there were those who saw what was happening to craftsmanship and good design and who started movements to go back to the best that had been lost, which they considered was not the furniture of the great designers of town furniture, but the traditional designs of country craftsmen. William Morris and the Cotswold School at the beginning of this century were some of those who tried to keep traditional styles and methods alive through the machine age. This is still done by various Guilds and schools of craftsmen today. Which is just as well for the many people wishing to furnish country homes today.

The continuity of country life

There is little doubt that the majority of the British people prefer the countryside to the town. 'Getting away from it all' usually means leaving town with as much haste as modern traffic allows, heading down the not so open road leading to fields, farms and cottages, for a day, a weekend, our annual holiday. If we reach the height of our ambitions, we buy our own country home, however small, to escape to whenever we can, or to live in permanently as soon as our circumstances allow.

Possessing two homes, one town and one country, isn't necessarily due to a modern desire for a status symbol; it is to satisfy a deep need for a way of life that has changed little over the centuries. The continuity of the countryside and all it contains is now the most secure and relaxing background a modern man can envisage. This is not so surprising when we realise that as late as the 19th century, Ebury Farm in London had stood for several centuries just behind what is now the Victoria Coach Station. Even Londoners must have had only a short journey to see country sights and sounds until a hundred years ago.

In 18th century France a French nobleman's idea of hell was to be banished from court life at Versailles to his country home. Englishmen built their greatest houses far from court in the countryside at this time, and what is more they lived in them, enriching the lives of all around them. Town houses for them have usually been a necessity, rather than a choice. Even the English court always preferred its rural retreats, hence the number of places claiming that 'Queen Elizabeth stayed here'.

Today we have a resurgence of the medieval wandering disease, combined with a deep desire to look backwards to find again what was best in the past, and what could be incorporated into present day life. Many of our farms and cottages are returning to the decoration and furnishings they were built to incorporate, restored with a greater knowledge than in the past and a greater understanding of the needs of country homes. Fireplaces are uncovered, unsightly wallpaper stripped off and panelling revealed, but what their owners are realizing is that even with modernization of plumbing and heating, what a country home needs above everything else is country furniture.

A-Z of
Farmhouse, Cottage and
Country Furniture

Alder (*Alnus glutinosa*) A native British and European tree. It is a hardwood, resistant to decay and used for turning, as in Windsor chairs, and tables. It is white when first cut, turning red and flesh colour later. In the 19th century it was easily stained to resemble mahogany and walnut.

AMERICAN COUNTRY FURNITURE

The first colonists of the eastern coast of North America, the Pilgrim Fathers, arrived in New England in 1620. They took with them the ideas in furnishing of the late Tudor and Jacobean styles, from the homes they had left behind in 17th century England.

Few actual pieces of furniture would have been carried over in the early years of colonization; and until craftsmen arrived, together with their tools, the minimum of furniture must have been made, of a purely utilitarian nature, from the wood at hand. This fundamental need underlay the designs of all the early furniture, even when conditions grew easier and more craftsmen were available to supply what was required. Fitness for purpose and durability are two of the essential characteristics of all country furniture, and when the Americans began to develop the designs they started out with from England, they adapted them to fit their particular needs. They made styles unknown in England. For example, they made wagon seats, double seats on a frame, usually wooden but sometimes rushed, which could be used both as a settee in the home and as a seat in a wagon.

American country furniture became the basis for much of the later furniture in the towns that grew up in the 18th century, whereas in England town and country furniture came to a parting of the ways at the end of the 17th century. In America several country pieces developed into styles that were acceptable in the homes of the highest in the land. Unhampered by heavy traditions, the country furniture of America seems to have found it easier to lighten its designs than its English counterparts. The Windsor chair is a good example. In England it remained a country or kitchen piece of rather staid design. In America, however, it became tall and elegant, and more comfortable, with greater splay to the legs, with headrests and with writing arms for ease in reading and writing. The New England fan-back, the writing Windsor, the double-comb Windsor giving a headrest, illustrate this very well. Instead of the heavier wooden settle, Windsor settees were made, a piece of furniture never popular in England.

When four poster beds were no longer fashionable, the Americans removed the tester and cut down the posts to the height of the headboard, and called it a low-post bed.

The rocking chair was an essentially American development, which eventually produced the Boston rocker, with elegant curves and painted designs, fit for any drawing room.

Although the early colonists found the oak tree in America and used this, they soon found it practicable to use the quantities of pine, maple, birch, walnut and hickory and the many fruitwoods, such as cherry, that they found growing in abundance near to hand. These woods were easier to work with and no doubt influenced their designs, for example, making curves and scrolls easier to produce than in solid oak.

For the most part the wood was left in its natural condition, acquiring colour and polish only with age and constant rubbing.

Immigrant influences The influences of the various nationalities that made up the different groups of settlers can be seen in the way the furniture was decorated. Painting was used more than carving, and much of the country furniture is very colourful. Panels on chests are often painted in the same designs as would have been used if the furniture had been carved.

Where carving has been used it has been possible to trace the designs on American chests and chairs to the area of their origin. The modern study of 17th century designs in both England and America is slowly revealing interesting information and comparisons as to their origin. (See *Carver* and *Chest* in the A–Z section.)

While the New England states were predominantly settled by the English, the Dutch settled in the New York/New Jersey area, and here is found the Dutch kas, the large wardrobe painted in colourful designs of fruit and flowers, and also painted dower chests.

The Swiss and German influence was strong in Pennsylvania, where painted furniture with much decoration and elaborate scrollwork was favoured. In particular the large storage wardrobe, the schrank, was a popular and much decorated prestige piece. The description 'Pennsylvania Dutch' applied to furniture of this area is a corruption of Deutsch (or German). The first German settlers came from the Rhineland and were invited over by William Penn at the end of the 17th century.

Further north in Quebec the craftsmen adapted the designs of 18th century France to the native softwoods of Canada, making the armoire, a large wardrobe, in designs inspired by furniture of the time of Louis XIII in Canadian softwoods.

In the south the Spanish influence was strong in New Mexico, California, Florida and Arizona, with a love of carving and leather. Texas was part of the Spanish colonies until the 19th century, when it was also populated by Germans, the isolated communities producing handmade furniture individually designed, usually in a massive style.

American designs The designs in American country furniture are usually plain but good, using many curves where English examples would have straight lines. The curved profiles at the sides of dressers and shelves, on chair and table aprons, give an elegant finish without a great deal of extra adornment being required.

If a piece of furniture was found useful it developed into some of the most highly decorated pieces in later town houses. This was the case with the high chest of drawers, the highboy, so popular that it was made in matching versions with the lowboy, the bottom half, used as an independent table.

Some uniquely American pieces obviously became popular because they were less elaborate in design than the English varieties. The simple version of the folding table, with butterfly wings for supports instead of gate-legs – easier to keep dusted, for one thing – and with widely splayed legs for extra stability is an example.

Probably American country furniture reached a peak in the 19th century with the furniture produced by the Shaker communities, when all that was best in simplicity, utility and craftsmanship went into its making.

The production of country furniture declined only, as it did in England, with the advent of the machine age.

America had its Arts and Crafts movement at the end of the 19th century, as did England in its William Morris era. The desire of its exponents for a return to the simple styles and craftsmanship of country furniture in the industrial age, eventually influenced 20th century furniture design.

One of the offshoots of this was the Mission style furniture of the early 1900s which resulted in the production of heavy oak furniture of rather crude design, based on the furniture of the Spanish Missions in Mexico. The style was extinct in 1913.

The American love of painted furniture continued in the industrially produced furniture of the 19th century. The Hitchcock chairs, settees and rocking chairs mass produced in Connecticut combined fashionable styles with country simplicity and had delicately painted and stencilled designs inspired by earlier Connecticut furniture.

Painted cottage furniture of the 19th century had long strips of applied ornament or spool turning as decoration, which was made possible by the invention of a multiple-bladed lathe, taking country designs well into the machine age.

(See also individual entries under *Chair, Chest of drawers, Chest, Children's furniture, Clock, Cupboard, Table, Settee* and *Shaker furniture.*)

Apple (*Malus pumila*) A very hard fruitwood, pinkish-brown in colour. It was popular for turned parts and used for much country furniture in both America and Europe, especially in the 17th and 18th centuries, instead of walnut and mahogany, when a lighter alternative to oak was wanted. It was also used for inlay work in the 17th century and for the cases of long-case clocks. It is susceptible to woodworm

Apron The shaped piece connecting the legs of tables just under the top; in chairs the piece beneath the seat rail; in a cabinet or dresser, along the base of the framework. It was often shaped or decorated with carving or pierced ornament. Sometimes its purpose was conceal-

Arcaded panel carving

ment of construction or in the case of close-chairs (*ie* commode chairs) concealment of the nature of the piece.

Arcading An arch supported on pillars, carved on a panel, popular in the late 16th and throughout the 17th century, used principally on chests, cupboards and chair backs (see figure).

Arcaded panels were often infilled with acanthus leaves or a palmated design (see *Palmated*) particularly popular in the western counties of England; or with stylized plant motifs or elaborate floral designs.

Chairs sometimes have the top back rail cut to resemble arches with pillars. This can be seen in some of the 17th century Yorkshire and Derbyshire chairs.

Ark This was a storage piece, made as early as the 13th century and still in use in the 19th. It was a large receptacle of split timber, hewn with an adze in early examples, with a canted or roof-shaped lid. It was made of oak or elm, not jointed but held together with wedges and pegs. Originally of North Country origin, it was used mainly in the kitchen to store flour, meal, grain and bread. Sometimes called a whitch or hutch and used with the description 'bolting' (meaning 'sifting') as in 'bolting hutch'. In Wales it is known as a coffer.

The 16th century Welsh example illustrated has a lid which when inverted may have been used as a handbarrow, with carrying poles inserted in the gabled ends (see figure).

A later example shown from Ipswich is of late 16th or early 17th century date, and is of panelled construction, with scratched mouldings running close to the sides of the stiles and rails, which are very wide. It can be dismantled for cleaning by withdrawing the pegs and wedges, thus making sure that no flour remains in the cracks. It has wooden pivot hinges, because iron might have tainted the flour (see photograph).

Arkwright A carpenter who made arks or heavy chests from split timber, using wedged and pegged construction.

Armoire
See *Cupboard*

Ark (late 16th or early 17th century) *Ipswich Museum*

Ark (Welsh; 16th century)

Ash (*Fraxinus excelsior*) The European ash belongs to a group that includes olive, lilac, privet and jasmine. The wood varies from light to medium brown. It is a tough wood of great elasticity, but subject to woodworm. It is used for turning, decorative veneers, drawer linings, the framework of furniture, and Windsor chairs, especially the stretchers and bows, as it bends well when steamed. It was also much used for farm carts and shafts and tool handles.

Aspen (*Populus tremula*) A wood light in both weight and colour used decoratively as veneer.

Aumbry
See *Cupboard*

Baby cage, baby walker or trotter This was an early type of playpen to keep a child contained and to help it to learn to walk. It consisted of two circular frames, the top much smaller than the bottom, held together with turned uprights, and usually with wheels to enable the child to push the cage around. The upper frame was often hinged so that it could be opened to put the child inside, the frame being small enough to prevent the child falling over and made to fit under its arms. Some walkers of this type had a small shelf round the top ring on which toys could be placed and an edge round the shelf to prevent them falling off. These date back to the 17th century (see figure).

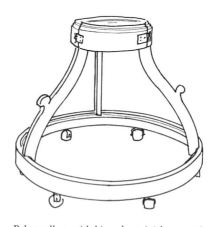

Baby walker, with hinged top (18th century)

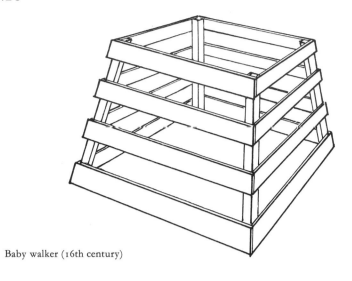

Baby walker (16th century)

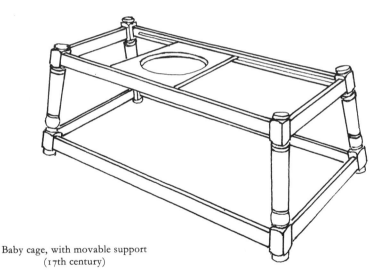

Baby cage, with movable support
(17th century)

Earlier cages dating back to the 16th century were square, with slatted sides, the slats either vertical or horizontal, with or without small wheels on the bottom (see figure).

Another 17th century model which was not movable consisted of an oblong wooden frame up to 2 m (about 6 ft) in length, with a sliding support for the child fitted into the top, enabling the baby to move backwards and forwards along the frame (see figure).

Back-stands (or back-stays) The two outside uprights which support the comb of a Windsor chair.

Ball foot A round, bulbous foot used in late 17th and early 18th century, to support chests, chests-of-drawers or tables (see figure). The term 'bun foot' is used to describe a foot of a flattened spherical shape.

Also sometimes known as 'onion foot'.

Ball turning
See *Bobbin turning*

Ball and ring turning A form of bobbin or ball turning with interspersed rings used in the late 17th century.
(See also *Turner*.)

Baluster A turned column, usually of classical form, used as a leg of a stool, table or chair from the late 16th and throughout the 17th century (see figure). Balusters carved with fluting were used in Elizabethan times. Baluster legs was the name given to the plain turned legs made by the bodgers for Windsor chairs, and to any plain spindle turnings. Baluster was also an alternative name for the back splat of a Windsor chair.
(See also *Turner*.)

Banding A decorative veneered border of contrasting wood used in the 18th century; when cut across the grain it is called cross banding.

Banister An alternate term for baluster.

Banker A cloth covering for a bench or back of a seat in the medieval period.

Barley sugar twist A form of turning that resembled a stick of barley sugar; it became popular in the reign of Charles II (see figure). It is seen on the legs and stretchers of tables,

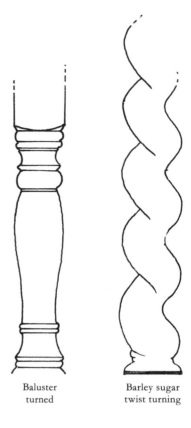

Baluster
turned

Barley sugar
twist turning

particularly gate-leg tables of the end of the 17th century, and on chairs. The early twists were partly turned and finished with handcarving, but a special device added to their lathes enabled the turners to produce a greater variety of spirals and twists on their lathes.
(See also *Turner*.)

Basketry This has long been used for various country articles such as corn measurers, beehives, baskets and trays but also for chairs and cradles, which have been made of coiled basketry for centuries. A chair of this type known as a *beehive* chair and a cradle of late 18th century date from Newbury in Berkshire are shown (see photograph, page 27). The cradle is worn at one corner suggesting continuous rocking by foot. It was still in use during the last century. Both the cradle and chair are made

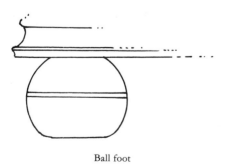

Ball foot

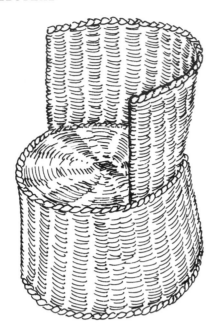

Wicker chair (Scottish)

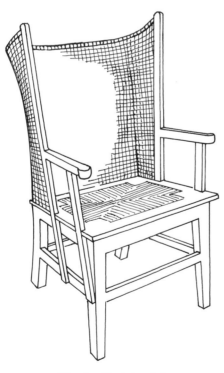

Wood and basketry chair
(Orkney)

of lip work, the name given to this coiled basketry, which is made of straw rope or 'lip', lashed and bound with strips of bramble, briar or holly bark.

Basket chairs are also known as wicker chairs, wanded chairs and 'twiggen' chairs, from the use of twigs (see figure).

In areas of Scotland such as the Islands and the western coasts, where wood was scarce, bent grass was used for basket work. Apart from chairs, the sides of food cupboards were ventilated with basket work; also wicker work coffins were made.

A chair that is still made in the Orkney Isles today has a wooden frame with a seat and back of basketry (see figure).

BEDSTEAD

Since for centuries people slept on floors, benches and chests, it is not surprising that by the end of the 15th century a bed when acquired was considered the most valuable piece of furniture in a home, not only for its comfort, but also for the richness of its hangings and bedding, on which the greater amount of money was spent. The decoration of the woodwork at this time was of secondary importance. The hangings were at first suspended from a canopy attached to the ceiling by cords. By about 1550 this became a wooden tester resting on four corner posts, with a panelled headboard. All that remains of these very early *four poster* or posted beds are some of the slender posts carved with geometrical ornament.

In the 16th century beds in the wealthier Tudor homes were heavily and richly carved, the decorative effort being transferred from the hangings to the woodwork, possibly because life in general was becoming more secure and furniture was less liable to be constantly uprooted. The tester was supported at the head on the panelled headboard and at the foot on two columns with large bulbous carvings. The bed frame itself was low and

Basketwork beehive chair and cradle (late 18th century)
Museum of English Rural Life, Reading

stood free at the foot on its own legs, attached to the framework at the head only. The side rails had holes for cords on which canvas or rush-matting was put (see figure overleaf).

By the 17th century four poster beds had posts of a more slender type, usually turned. A late 18th century oak bed from Anglesey is illustrated with the hangings removed to show its structure (see figure overleaf). It is of a type sometimes known as a *tent* bed which was also popular in 18th century America.

Some *half-headed* bedsteads, mentioned in many inventories had a panelled head only about 1.20 m (4 ft) high and no tester. A bed dated 1700 in Dorchester Museum, which came from a Dorset cottage, has the headboard and end legs of oak and the sides and end boards of elm. It still has its rush mattress, probably made in nearby Purbeck by craftsmen working the local sedge. Another name for bedsteads with headboard but no footboard was *stump-end* bedsteads. Beds without testers in America were known as *low-post beds*.

Humbler beds Poorer homes often had *boarded* beds, open boxes with a straw or feather mattress. These persisted in many country areas throughout the 18th century. Others may

BEDSTEAD

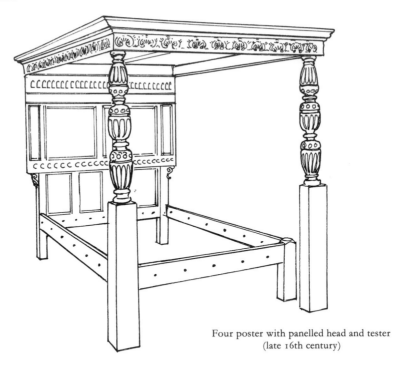

Four poster with panelled head and tester
(late 16th century)

'Tent bed' (Welsh; late 18th century)

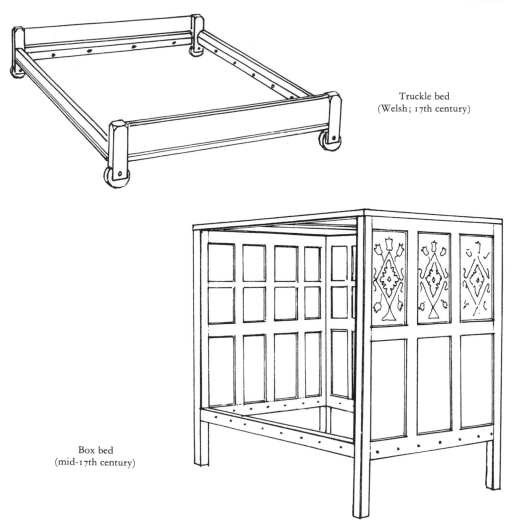

Truckle bed
(Welsh; 17th century)

Box bed
(mid-17th century)

have had the bed frame only supported on legs, sometimes called a *stump* bedstead, again with holes drilled in the sides, head and foot to take cords which supported the mattress.

Inventories show that by 1600 even the labouring classes had bedsteads, and in 1656 a yeoman farmer was able to leave to his wife 'One posted bedstead with mattress, curtains and valance, feather bed, bolster and two pillows, two blankets and a coverlet'. Beds always take pride of place in old wills and inventories, being the one item of furniture associated with the most important moments in life, from birth to death.

Many beds were built into cupboard recesses in cottages and farmhouses to save space, often under staircases.

From medieval times to the 18th century many larger beds had a *truckle* or *trundle* bed; this was a small bed on wheels with a frame containing holes for cording for a mattress (see figure). This could be pushed under the larger bed when not in use, for a servant or child. Such a bed is shown at the American Museum at

Press bedstead, closed position (Pembrokeshire, early 19th century)
and (below) the same bedstead, open position   *National Museum of Wales*

Bath, underneath the four poster bed in the 'Borning Room', a small room in an early American home, which was situated near the kitchen for convenience and used in time of childbirth or illness.

Various types of *folding* beds have always been popular in country houses to save space. An early 18th century American room, also at Bath, has a large pine folding bed with wooden hinges and hangings of home-spun linen embroidered in bright crewel-work. The same cords threaded through the frame support the feather mattress as in England. A similar folding bed design appears in Loudon's 19th century book of country furniture designs, where there is also a drawing of a *box* bedstead, a 'room within a toom' type with panels on three sides and curtains on the open side, popular for many years in cold bedrooms. These could be used to divide a living room into sections for night and day use, and are still found in old cottages, the backs often fitted with shelves (see figure, page 29).

Another type shown in Loudon's book used in homes with limited accommodation in the 18th and early 19th centuries was the *press* bedstead, capable of being folded up and concealed in a small press or chest of drawers. An example from Pembrokeshire of the early 19th century is shown in both the open and closed position (see photographs).

Camp beds have a long history and as *trussing beds*, capable of being easily dismantled for travelling, with their hangings, survived well into the 16th century, and as camp beds appeared in 19th century design books.

Beech (*Fagus sylvatica*) This wood has always been popular for country furniture, especially for turned parts, although it is subject to woodworm. It is also used for toolmaking. It polishes well to a light brown colour, varying to reddish brown, and is easily worked. It bends easily when steamed and the common Windsor chair was usually made of turned parts of beech with an ash bow and elm seat. The main centre of production at High Wycombe in Buckinghamshire relied on the beech trees that have grown in the Chilterns since pre-historic times. The flinty clay soil over the chalk enabled it to grow in profusion, until it became known as the Buckinghamshire weed. Beech cuts smoothly while still green and can then be left to dry for a considerable period without warping or cracking, so it was well suited to the making of chair legs by the bodgers working the woods in this area (see *Bodger*).

When English walnut became scarce at the end of the 17th century many carved chairs were made in beech, but it was also used for the frames of upholstered chairs and stools, and for painted furniture, especially chairs of the late Georgian period that were often stained to look like mahogany.

Bench A long seat with or without a back. The most usual form of seating in medieval times at long trestle tables, when it was either free standing or fixed to the wall. Early benches were of the same trestle construction as the tables. A Welsh example from Monmouthshire is illustrated of 15th century date,

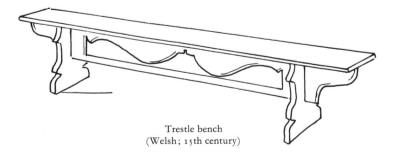

Trestle bench
(Welsh; 15th century)

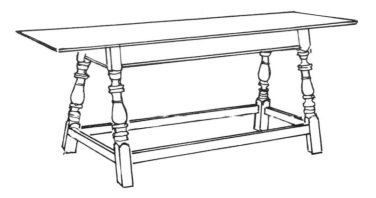

Oak bench (Welsh; late 17th century)

with Gothic shaped ends and pierced under-framing (see figure). This oak example is typical of the benches used by the gentry until the end of the 17th century and up to the present day in many farmhouses. A later 17th century example with turned supports joined by stretchers is also illustrated (see figure).

Benchman A woodworker in a small country town or village workshop, responsible for using a bow or frame saw. In particular, he provided the blank elm seats for Windsor chairs for the bottomer to shape.

Bender The craftsman who made the bow backs and curved stretchers of Windsor chairs, the best of which were made of yew or ash stakes, the rest of bows sawn from a plank, all roughly shaped with a draw-knife before

bending. Each bow had to be steamed or boiled in a tank of water until pliable and then bent on a bending table, where it was pegged into the correct position round a shaping block and left to dry. When it was moved from the table a strut was fitted to keep it in position. Some experienced workers were able to bend a bow by hand, the two ends being tied together in position with a cord.

Billet The roughly shaped leg of a chair cut from the sawn lengths of tree trunk, ready to be turned on the lathe.

Birch (*Betula alba*) A native British tree, but many varieties are found elsewhere in temperate zones. The wood is light reddish brown with silvery streaks and was sometimes used as a cheap substitute for satinwood in the late 18th century. Birch is used in making the cheaper types of furniture and plywood. It bends easily when steamed. Harder varieties have greater strength and polish well to look like imitations of mahogany and walnut. It was imported from North America after 1750.

Black oak
See *Bog oak*

Bobbin turning A succession of small balls or bobbins used on turned legs and stretchers in the 17th century (see figure).

Bobbin
turning

Bobtail A small extension on the back of a Windsor chair seat into which bracing sticks are socketed (see figure).

BODGER

A craftsman who made the legs, back spindles and stretchers for Windsor chairs; he sometimes worked for himself or was employed by a farmer, doing the work in between other seasonal employment. The bodger would move from one place to another in the woods, and was to be found particularly in the beech woods of the High Wycombe district of Buckinghamshire. Here he survived until the early 1950s, when he was at last replaced by factory methods and modern machinery; the last of his line, Owen Dean of Great Hampden ending the tradition of five hundred years. The photograph overleaf shows him at work.

The bodger would buy a stand of trees, enough to keep him employed for a year or longer in the same wood, set up his portable shelter, and select those trees best suited to his purpose, straight grained and of quick growth.

The bodgers worked alongside the tree fellers in the woods, sometimes cutting down the trees they had purchased themselves.

After felling, the trunks were trimmed with an axe and sawn into 45 cm (18 in) lengths, with a cross-cut saw. The lengths were then cleft with a beetle and wedge into as many chair leg pieces or billets as possible, sometimes four, sometimes sixteen. Such hand-split legs were well thought of as being stronger and less liable to warp than those cut by machines. They were then reduced to the rough outline of a chair leg with a few strokes of a small side axe, or metal froe (see *Tools*), and further shaped with a draw-knife.

To do this the craftsman sat astride a shavehorse, which held the piece of wood to be shaved in a clamp, pulling the draw-knife held in both hands towards him, and shaping the leg as near as possible to its finished shape, to reduce the amount of turning to be done. The leg was then turned on a pole-lathe (see *Tools*), a type that has been in use since Iron Age times, a V-shaped chisel being used to form the

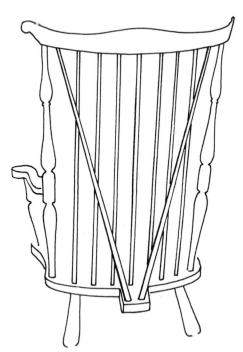

Bobtail and bracing sticks

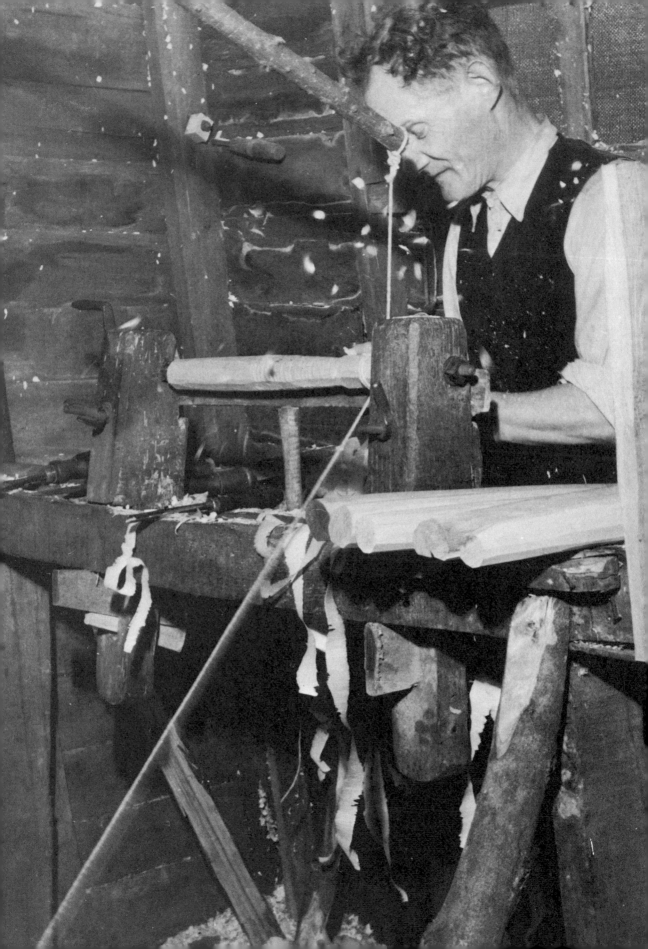

various shapes of turning. The whole turning process took about two minutes.

The legs were turned while the wood was still green, and stacked to dry for weeks before being sent to factories where benchmen and framers completed the chairs.

The reason why the bodgers worked this way in the woods was that it was easier and cheaper for them to take their equipment to the trees, than it was for the trees to be transported to the workshops. There was a considerable amount of tree left when the parts suitable for turning had been selected, and when the bodgers had finished with them, others could take the remaining wood for their own particular needs. Some was taken to be sawn into planks and chair seats, some for kindling wood, and some for the charcoal burners who also worked in the forests.

The name bodger is of uncertain origin and may not have been used for these workmen until the present century, perhaps in a slightly disparaging way by other workers in the chair industry; to 'bodge up' means to put together or patch up clumsily. *The Shorter Oxford English Dictionary* suggests that the word is a variant of badger, a travelling pedlar, and the bodgers did in fact often travel around selling their finished legs and stretchers.

Bog oak Sometimes called 'black oak'. This wood is obtained from oak that has been buried in a peat bog. It is very dark in colour, resembling ebony.

Bookcase The library of an average cottage or farmhouse until the 19th century could no doubt have been contained in a box, such as a Bible box, or desk, or on a small set of hanging bookshelves. Bookcases as such were built into many wealthier country houses by local joiners and are of excellent workmanship.

Boss A knob-like ornament used as a decoration, often an applied, split decoration in the 17th century.

(See *Split-turned ornaments*.)

Bottomer The craftsman who was responsible for shaping the seats of Windsor chairs, from the blank elm seats, some 45 cm (18 in) square and 5 cm (2 in) thick, with an adze; work today done by machines.

Bow A curved member of a Windsor chair, made of wood that can be steamed and bent to the required shape of a back bow or armed bow.

BOX

A container for storage, and in the case of country furniture, made of wood. It was an article mentioned in many inventories, without further description, and which obviously came in all shapes and sizes; it was used for many purposes rarely indicated by the simple term 'box'. Modern box files are a continuation of one of the earliest uses of a box, to store and classify important papers.

Bible box In the 17th century a type of box appears which in Victorian times became known as a Bible box. The newly published Authorised Version of the Bible was found in almost every Stuart houshold and held in high regard. Although these boxes may have been used for other purposes, they are often elaborately decorated with carving or incised or scratched decoration, so that it is more than likely that they were regarded as important and used for the storage of what may have been the one and only book owned by the family, which was also used as the family register for the recording of births, marriages and deaths. One type had a sloping top (see overleaf) forming a bookrest at the daily Bible readings.

The other type was simply a rectangular box with decoration along the front (see figure). In the 17th century the decoration was often a strip of continuous pattern, perhaps ending in the middle of the design.

Boxes of similar date and design are found in America. The box illustrated is of late 17th

The bodger, at his pole-lathe
Museum of English Rural Life, Reading

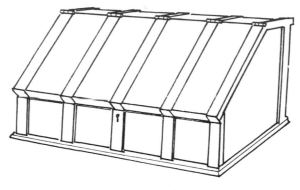

Bible box (Jacobean)

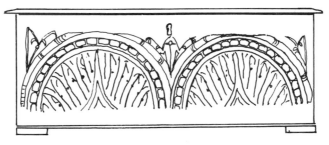

Bible box (17th century)

American Bible box (late 17th century)
Old Sturbridge Village, Massachusetts

century date and comes from Old Sturbridge Village, Massachusetts. It has the same flat relief carving of flowers and leaves as is found on the Hadley chests from this district (see photograph). In Wales a unique form of Bible box is found in the '*y coffer bach*' or the little coffer. This is usually made in oak or elm, occasionally inlaid with holly, and found chiefly in the south western part of Wales. It takes the form of a small edition of the mule chest (see *Chest of drawers*). Most examples date from the second half of the 18th century. The upper chest part has a panelled front and the lower section has one or two drawers to hold important family papers.

There is a certain tradition that in Wales these small coffers were 'love chests' and filled with fine linen were part of a bride's dowry. Many were made in the family circle during long winter evenings, until as late as the mid-19th century. In their book *Welsh Furniture*, L. Twiston-Davies and H. J. Lloyd-Johnes warn that 'Intending purchasers should try to obtain some pedigree with their pieces, as the "coffer bach" was copied frequently in the period between the wars, and when made of old wood is very difficult to date'.

Bible boxes were made in both town and country, but many country boxes were obviously homemade and often dated, sometimes having the date and initials of the maker on the lid in brass or iron studs.

Some unusually long boxes may have been used for such small articles of clothing as lace or gloves. These types were used as 'lace chests' by the lacemakers in Buckinghamshire and other lacemaking districts.

Bobbin box A small box used by lacemakers to keep bobbins in when not in use.

Book box This was carved in the outward form of a book, occasionally made to contain a Bible, and sometimes actually contrived out of a real book, with a cavity inside to hide papers or small objects.

Candle box These were usually cylindrical in shape with a curved lid, often with leather hinges and were hung horizontally on the wall. They were made of many different woods and often decorated with carvings or paintings. Metal examples also exist. Another type had the advantage that the candles were kept in an upright position in a rectangular box with a sliding front, which lifted upwards and enabled the candles to be removed without damage; this design prevented them sticking together, as they might if placed lying on top of each other. Candles were an important household item and were also stored on small hanging shelves with fronts to prevent the candles falling off.

Desk box
See *Desk*

Knife box These mostly date from the late 18th century onwards and hung vertically on the wall. Made of various woods, they were

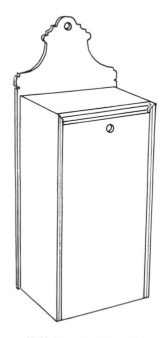

Knife box with sliding lid

deep enough for the knives to stand upright, the large handles uppermost, the side of the box tapering to conform with the shape of the knives. In one type the lid was at the top and sloped sharply; it had metal hinges. The purpose of the box was occasionally made clear by designs of a knife and fork inlaid in boxwood on the front of the box.

Another type had a sliding lid at the front, fitting into grooves at the sides (see figure).

Pipe box These were long rectangular boxes, hung vertically on walls, very like a knife box but with an open top, which held the long 18th century pipes and tapers. They had small drawers in the base for tobacco.

Plate box Country-made cutlery trays or boxes of 18th century date or later were made, with divisions for the various items of cutlery. Early examples have a handle cut out of the central partition for lifting; later examples usually have metal handles.

Salt box This wooden box of oak or sycamore, with leather hinges to prevent corrosion by the salt, hung on the cottage or farmhouse wall near the fireplace, to keep the precious salt dry. Salt boxes were usually rectangular in shape, wider than knife boxes and with straight parallel sides; they also had a sloping hinged lid. They date from Elizabethan times.

Spice box
See *Cupboard*

Boxwood (*Buxus semper-virens*) A hard, pale yellow wood growing in Britain, Europe and Asia, used for turned parts and decorative inlays and for carving.

Bracing sticks The supports which extend from the bow to the bob-tail at the rear of the seat of a Windsor chair (see figure, page 33).

Bracket A projection from a vertical member of a piece of furniture forming a support as on the underside of a folding table (see figure).

Bracket foot A foot used in much 18th century furniture, such as chests of drawers, made of two pieces of wood joined at right angles, and strengthened with a piece of wood glued inside the angle. The foot was then fastened to the corner of the frame. The wood was cut to a decorative outline (see figure). When curved to a serpentine shape it was known as an ogee foot.

Bread (or kneading) trough or dough bin This was a form of chest made of oak or elm, 1.50–1.80 m (5–6 ft) long, with splayed sides and splayed legs, which held flour or dough in separate compartments (see figure). It was a common article in country kitchens of the 17th and 18th century. It had a lid,

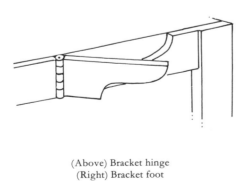

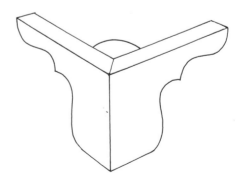

(Above) Bracket hinge
(Right) Bracket foot

Bread trough or dough bin

sometimes hinged, which served as a table top for breadmaking or as an ironing board.

In Loudon's *Encyclopaedia* of 1833 he describes this piece of furniture as one of the most economical of kitchen tables, 'such as are a good deal in use in the cottages and small farmhouses in many parts of England.'

Brown figured oak This is wood from a tree with a slight decay causing variegated rich brown streaks. Very beautiful, but it cannot bear a great strain, so is suited to interior work in houses and some furniture. It does not need to be darkened or treated with polish.

Bulbous The term applied to the large turned ornaments on legs, bedposts and court cupboard supports in the Elizabethan period, often melon shaped or carved in 'cup and cover' designs (see *Cup and cover*). They were made by gluing four sections to the leg to be turned, before it was turned into the bulbous form. They were of Flemish origin and were still used in the 17th century in plainer, uncarved forms.

See also *Turner*.

Bun foot
See *Ball foot*

Bureau This is a development of the early desk (see *Desk*) with a sloping top, on a stand or table, which eventually became a desk on a chest of drawers. The desk top instead of opening upwards, with a hinge on the top, now opened downwards to form a writing table resting on two lopers (supporting arms) which pulled out at the sides. The hinges were now at the bottom.

Many of these bureaux were made in oak for country homes in the 18th and 19th centuries, the top being fitted with a variety of small pigeon holes and drawers. An extension to the top of the bureau giving a cabinet or bookcase with solid panelled doors was made in the 18th century, and while many pieces were made in walnut and mahogany by cabinet makers in towns, the country craftsmen did their best to make the piece in oak, without the curves and veneering used by the 18th century cabinet maker. The example illustrated is of Queen Anne date; it has the bracket feet and fielded panels of the period (see figure overleaf).

Bureau bookcase ('Queen Anne')

Burr A growth on a tree which gives elaborately marked wood suitable for decorative purposes *eg*, burr elm, or burr yew, alder, maple or walnut.

Buttonwood The American plane tree; the wood is reddish brown in colour and is used principally for chairs.

Cabriole leg This is a curved leg used on chairs, cabinets and tables, introduced into England in the William and Mary period, taking its name from the French for the leaping movement, or caper of a goat; alternatively sometimes called a bandy leg. It is not turned on the lathe but is made from a square of wood cut down to the required shape by the cabinet maker on the bench. The top of the leg curves outwards, then inwards in an S-shape to end in a foot, rounded, square-shaped or hoof-

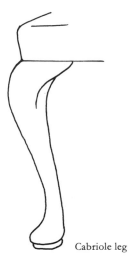
Cabriole leg

and children, often boys and girls only seven years old, wove the cane into a great variety of patterns, using an old knife for cutting, a mallet to drive in the pegs to which the cane was attached and a few awl-like pegs for clearing holes.

Rush matting was also used for seat bottoms Again the workers were women who did this dirty and smelly work on the workshop floor, sorting and plaiting the rushes which had to be soaked in water to make them pliable. The work was considered so unhealthy that in the latter half of the 19th century the Wycombe matters had to undergo a monthly medical examination. Rush-seated chairs were popular throughout the 18th and 19th centuries.

Caning was used for chair seats and backs from the Restoration period onwards. A large mesh was used in earlier chairs, becoming smaller towards the end of the 17th century, when the cane chairmaker was established as a specialized independent craftsman in towns. The demand for their light cheap chairs, especially after the Great Fire of London in 1666, caused trouble with other chair makers, in particular the makers of the more expensive upholstered chairs. A petition to suppress the cane chair industry was however unsuccessful.

When mechanization took over much of the lacemaking industry, many of the cottagers who had formerly made lace turned their hand to seat caning (see photograph overleaf).

Cane furniture again became popular in Victorian times.

Caning can still be done at home by anyone wishing to re-cane an old chair seat. The cane can be bought at craft centres and comes in various thicknesses. These are numbered according to size; the sizes normally used for chairs are numbers 2 and 3, or 2 and 4. Craft books can be bought showing a variety of patterns which can be followed. The most usual is called Standard Double Setting which gives six layers of cane covering the seat, woven in and out of each other. The cane has to be soaked for a short time before being used to

shaped (see figure). On the legs made by cabinet makers in towns more elaborate feet appear and a decorated leg bracket was used, which softened and disguised the point at which the legs joined the underside of the chair seat.

For country craftsmen it was a difficult shape to achieve in oak, to enable the leg to appear as a harmonious part of the whole piece of furniture. In much country work it looks as if added later as an afterthought. But the leg was used in country work, especially in Windsor chairs of the mid-18th century and is used to best effect in the Chippendale Windsor Chairs popular from 1770 to the mid-19th century in some districts, long after the cabriole leg had gone out of fashion in town furniture. The leg was re-introduced in the Windsor chairs made by Jack Goodchild in the present century.

(See also Windsor chairs, in the *Chair* section.)

CANER, CANING AND RUSH MATTING

Traditionally a caner in country districts was a woman working in her own home; caning was a cottage industry. The actual preparation of the canes was done by men, who cut and split the canes and removed the pith. The women

make it easy to weave, and kept wrapped in a cloth to keep it pliable while working. The only tools needed are a sharp knife or scissors to cut the cane, a bodkin and a few pegs to hold the canes firmly in the holes while weaving. *Note* Instructions are given in Dryad Leaflet no. 16: *Cane and Rush Seating*, price 20p; this is available from Reeves Dryad, 178 Kensington High Street, London W8.

Canted The sides or arms of a piece of furniture set at a slope (see figure).

CARPENTER

Throughout the Middle Ages the carpenter was the most important of the craftsmen working in wood. He spent most of his time making the timber frames of medieval houses, as well as farm buildings and implements. Only when not engaged in this work did he make simple sturdy pieces of furniture, and only very occasionally did he find time to decorate it with simple chip carving or scratched designs (see *Carver* and *Scratch carving*).

The earliest wood used was not sawn but was split by the carpenters with iron and wooden wedges and trimmed with an adze (see *Tools*). The marks of the adze can be seen on much of this early riven timber. Where later the trunk was sawn up in layers into planks, without being split first into sections, not only did the planks gradually diminish in width from the centre of the trunk outwards, but this method also produced wood with very uninteresting grain patterns. However it is thought that a great deal of early furniture was produced by carpenters from planks sawn in this way (see *Sawyer*).

Carpenters joined the pieces of furniture they made with hand-wrought nails or wooden pegs. No glue was used; its use was forbidden by the carpenters' Guilds which were in existence from the 12th century onwards. While country carpenters were not controlled by these Guilds, many would have had their training either under the control of

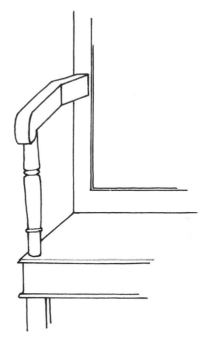

A canted chair arm

the Guilds which operated in London and other large towns, or in monastic establishments throughout the country which were responsible for so much medieval building.

Apart from this, the majority of country carpenters would have acquired their training from their fathers, using methods and designs that had stood the test of time.

They were able to make mortise and tenon joints (see *Joints*) but only on a massive scale in structural work. The large mortises were bored with an auger and the tenons cut with a bow saw (again, see *Tools*). A hole was bored through the assembled joint and a wooden peg driven in. Smaller joints were cut with a chisel.

Carpenters' pieces Carpenters made slab-sided chests and cupboards, and stools and benches of a simple type with legs fitted into holes bored in the seats. They made large table tops supported on trestles, joined by one or two stretcher rails, which passed through the

43

Seat caning: a cottage industry
Museum of English Rural Life, Reading

trestles, protruded each end and were fastened with a large peg or wedge. These tables which had matching benches and stools could be dismantled when they needed to be moved.

Most of the few articles of furniture required in medieval homes until the 15th century were made by carpenters. The drawback to the furniture they produced was that it was heavy and inclined to split across the grain and warp. The wood could not move as it could under the later panel and frame construction of the joiner introduced in the 15th century. The planks were held rigidly in position by the nails and pegs.

The joiners eventually took over furniture making, although country carpenters were still making chests and boxes using plank construction as late as the 18th century.

Carpets and other floor coverings A carpet was originally a piece of woven material or tapestry used for covering tables, shelves and cupboards. No one would have dreamed of putting a carpet on a medieval floor, which was covered only with rushes, herbs and hay. Various accounts by eye-witnesses describe these 16th century or earlier floors as varying from clean and sweet smelling to positively disgusting, no doubt depending on the diligence of the housewife and the frequency of changing the rushes. In the 17th and 18th centuries plaited rush matting would have been used. Although woven knotted pile carpets were being made in England by this time, their price would have been beyond the reach of most country homes.

Clip rugs and rag mats For several centuries clip-rugs or rag-mats have been made by country housewives from clippings of cloth of various colours sewn together on strong canvas or sacking. This made a strong, hardwearing rug of comfortable thickness. These are also known as 'hooked' rugs in America and 'pegged' or 'hooked' rugs in Britain.

They probably originated in the north of England as protection from cold stone floors, when housewives made them from left-over pieces of wool from northern mills. Similar rugs are made today from rug wool.

For the most part rag rugs were made in cottages and farmhouses from the contents of the household rag bag cut into strips either pushed through the canvas with a peg, the two ends pulled through the loop made; or else by pulling the loop of rag through with a hook, and hooking it through the two cut ends as in crochet work. The rug is often sheared or clipped to make an even finish.

CARVER AND CARVING

During the 13th to 15th centuries woodcarvers were principally employed in work in churches and cathedrals. Most of the furniture they did have time to carve was decorated in a style known as 'Gothic', although this actual term was not used until Tudor times, and then only as a term of abuse. The style was based on the tracery shapes of windows and arches which the carver saw around him in cathedrals and churches. Areas of the country that have fine timberwork in their churches also produced domestic furniture with carving of superior quality. This is apparent in counties such as Somerset, Norfolk and Suffolk. Many pieces of this early furniture, carved for domestic use, can now be seen in local parish churches, as when it eventually became unfashionable in country homes – something that did not in fact happen for many years – it was often donated by its owners to the churches that had originally inspired the designs.

Early types of carving The oak of which most early furniture was made was not easy to carve, and the carving was of a bold and rough quality. It was done with chisel and gouge, the marks of which are often visible.

Early *chip carving* was done either by

removing the pattern from the surface of the wood, or in the case of sunk carving, the background was removed, leaving the pattern on the face of the chest or cupboard being carved. The patterns were often geometrical; perhaps a series of half round channels would be gouged out of the wood, usually along a frieze. The simplest form of incised or *scratch carving* was merely lines scratched on the surface. This is found in use up to the early 18th century. When the pattern was part of a food cupboard the tracery patterns were cut right through to act as ventilation holes.

Continental influences During the reign of Henry VIII craftsmen were imported from the Continent to work on the King's palaces, and for the first time English carvers saw some of the classically-based designs of the European Renaissance, which appeared on the furniture of the time in panels on chests and chairs, with profile medallioned heads, vases and scrolls. The English craftsmen used these designs without much knowledge or appreciation of the classical thought behind them, and under the Tudors carving became more and more flamboyant and unrestrained. Strapwork of arabesques, geometrical interlacing and chain patterns was popular, together with masks and grotesques, arcading on panels or a series of arches, flutes and lunettes (see individual entries on these). After Henry's break with the Catholic church, Italian workmen no longer came to England, but continental influences continued to reach England through Flemish craftsmen who came to work in English houses.

The fact that so many craftsmen who had formerly worked for the church were freed at this time to make and design without regard to their religious masters also accounted for this explosion of such a great variety of designs. Their customers and patrons were now the newly enriched yeomen farmers and merchants, who wanted furniture that reflected the increased prosperity of their lives.

The continental motifs were copied by country craftsmen from the work they saw in the great country houses being decorated around them. These they used in an uninhibited mixture with traditional Gothic designs, how and when the craftsman or his client wanted them, reaching a climax of exuberance in the reign of Elizabeth I. This is shown particularly in the supports of Elizabethan cupboards, table legs and bedposts, which after being turned were heavily carved with ionic capitals, cup and cover forms (see *Cup and cover*) on the large bulbous and melon shapes, and acanthus leaves. Some of this carving was done by joiners and some by specialist carvers. The carvers were usually members of the joiners guilds, but the joiners were principally concerned with structure and the carvers with decoration.

One of the most popular ways of carving the panels of 16th century chests, chair backs and wall panelling was with the *linenfold* pattern (see *Linenfold*). This was of Flemish origin and generally thought to be based on the folds of a piece of linen. There may have been a more practical reason for its use. Early riven oak was liable to have ridges in it and these may have suggested the lines of the folded linen. In any case the edges of the panels had to be reduced to fit into the frames, and the craftsman may have adapted the design to suit both his needs and the natural formation of the wood.

17th century chests and chairs were still carved with simple gouge cuts, lunettes and arcaded panels, also diamond-shaped lozenges (see *Lozenge*). Early 17th century plank chests were sometimes carved to look as if they were of panel and frame construction.

Regional design The large numbers of chests and chairs dating from the first half of the 17th century still in existence provides a large field for modern furniture research. This is still in its early stages and has been pioneered in this country by Temple Newsam House Museum, Leeds. By studying the carving of this period in various areas, a pattern is beginning to emerge of the designs favoured in different parts of England, before designs became standardized by the publication of pattern books in the 18th century, by improved communications and by the spread of industrialization in the 19th century.

The allocation of particular designs to particular areas is being much helped by research going on at the same time in America, into designs on early furniture in the American colonies. These colonies had little communication with each other in the early days of settlement due to remoteness. They had more connection with the places they had left in England, so it is easier to isolate various designs in America than it is here, where there has always been more movement in the population, and designs were dispersed over the country at an early date.

Early regional designs are also easier to identify in America through the analysis of woods used. Many of their trees grew only in specific regions, unlike Britain where most varieties are dispersed over the whole country.

It has already been found that some motifs on 17th century American chests and chairs are almost identical to those found in England, helping to pinpoint English sources with greater accuracy. An example is the double heart motif attributed to the Guildford area of New Haven colony, which is found here chiefly in Gloucestershire and the West Country.

Post-Restoration The coming of the Commonwealth period brought a severe restriction of the carver's work. All carving was frowned upon by the Puritans, and most furniture decoration at this time was done by the turners. By the time carving returned to fashion after the Restoration in 1660 designs had become more restrained and delicate. The carver's attention in the second half of the 17th century was largely focused on chairs. He carved the stretchers and arcaded backs of the types that originated in Yorkshire and Derbyshire and later in the highly decorated chairs that became so popular in the reign of Charles II. The increase in the use of walnut made the carver's work much easier and he was able to produce the pierced designs required by these cane-seated types, helping to give them the lightness now required. Carving reached the very summit of craftsmanship with the intricate work of Grinling Gibbons, carver to Charles II, who working in limewood carved such wonderful flowers and foliage.

As far as the work of the country carver was concerned, he continued for the most part using 17th century designs throughout the 18th century. The date of 1660 which brought such changes in styles to town cabinet makers exerted little influence in the countryside.

The Gothic revival The next great period for carving was in the Victorian age, when again the increased wealth of a new section of the population resulted in a wave of highly decorated furniture, as it had in Elizabethan times. This time the wealth was due to the new industrial age, but unfortunately this time professional and amateur carvers alike carved everything in sight during a revival of exaggerated Gothic styles and romantic furniture, resulting from the popularity of the works of such writers as Sir Walter Scott. One result of this was the furniture known as 'Abbotsford', taking its name from the home of Scott. Unfortunately the Victorians carved a large quantity of the plainer oak pieces of earlier days, such as Welsh chests. This is a factor to be taken into account when dating country furniture.

(See also *Chain motif; Cup and cover; Double heart motif; Guilloche; Grotesque; Rope carving; Rosette; Scratch carving; Strapwork; Sunk carving.*)

Carver's wood Another name for the wood of the lime tree, extensively used by woodcarvers. Most of the work done by Grinling

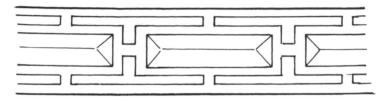

Chain motif, used in carving

Gibbons (1648–1721), carver to Charles II, was executed in lime. He specialized in the carving of intricate designs and foliage, birds, fruit and shells.

Cedar The aromatic wood of the cedar tree has long been popular for use in chests, drawers and cupboards where clothes, blankets and linen were to be stored. Apart from the sweet smell the wood is also said to be a protection against moths. The red cedar used in America is the *Juniperus virginiana* of North America and the *Cedrela odorata* of the West Indies. The cedar of Lebanon (*Cedrus libanotica*) was introduced into England in the 17th century.

Another aromatic wood, that of the cypress (*Cupressus*) was used for similar purposes; it was introduced into this country in the 16th century.

Chain motif A form of strapwork carving which had a widespread use throughout the 16th and 17th centuries as a decoration on oak furniture. It consisted of rectangular linked chains, or alternately carved round and rectangular linked chains (see figure). It was frequently used in the west of England, principally along stiles and rails of chests.

CHAIR

Armchair A chair with arms was one of the earliest types of chairs. It was in use in medieval times and until the 16th century very scarce and reserved for the head of the household and his important guests. The chair was a symbol of importance and authority, as can still be seen in the position of a 'chairman' today, or in the Speaker's Chair in the House of Commons where, as in medieval times, the rest of the company occupy benches. After the 15th century these chairs were joined or joint chairs. They were made by joiners and had boxed-in, panelled seats, backs and arms. They were sometimes called wainscot chairs, although this term referred to the wood (oak) from which the chair was made and not to the design (see *Wainscot*). They were heavy and were seldom moved from the place of importance they occupied. A modern term for this type is 'panel-back'.

Early armchairs made by turners are shown by medieval manuscripts to have existed from a very early date (see *Turned chair* later in this section).

Another early type is the X-chair made by coffermakers (see *Cofferer*).

Joined chairs

Joined chairs became more plentiful as the 16th century progressed, and as they did so it was necessary for them to become lighter in construction and more movable. The panels beneath the seat and arms consequently gave way to turned front legs and arm supports, and square back legs and stretchers. The back panel in the best examples was decorated with carving or inlaid panels of coloured woods. Holes in the front of the seats of these early chairs indicate that they held ropes supporting a cushion. Some of the wooden seats may have been added later.

In the 16th century the top rail of the

47

panelled back was fixed between the uprights and tenoned into them. In the 17th century it often became a cresting (carved decorative rail) with the uprights tenoned into it, or with the cresting extended on either side. The chair illustrated (see figure) is about 1670 in date and comes from Wales. It has a scrolled cresting and brackets attached to the sides carved with conventional foliage. The back panel is decorated with a lozenge motif. Much of the carving on these 17th century chairs was of similar designs to that on chests of the same date (see *Chest* and *Carver and carving*). The stretchers are placed near the ground, both to add strength to the chair and to provide protection for the feet from cold and rush-strewn floors.

Another type of 17th century armchair is described later in this section under *Caquetoire*.

Panel-back armchairs were still being made throughout the 18th century in country areas.

The illustration shows one from Wales of about 1720–30 date, which has fielded panels and a drawer beneath the seat (see figure). In America these armchairs are known as 'great chairs'.

Also of 18th century date is the armchair from Reading Museum shown in the photograph which is believed to have come from Shropshire. It shows a type of chair made in country areas on the lines of the earliest 'dug-out' chests, where the chair is carved out of a tree trunk and fitted with arms and seat. Probably a hollow tree was used, as in the case of the later Yorkshire example (see figure overleaf) which has had castors fitted; this is now in Lancaster Museum.

Ladder-back and spindle-back chairs in the 18th century were made as armchairs. The term 'elbow chair' was used at the end of the 17th century to distinguish the armchair in a set of dining chairs from the single chairs. This

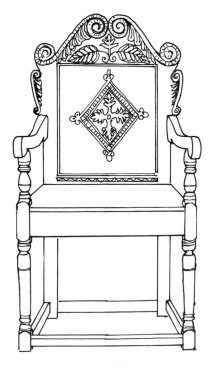

Oak armchair (Welsh; *c.*1670)

Armchair with drawers (Welsh; *c.*1720–30)

Armchair of dug-out type from Shropshire (18th century)
Museum of English Rural Life, Reading

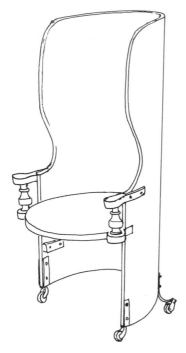

'Dug-out' chair, probably made from a hollow tree (Yorkshire)   *Lancaster Museum*

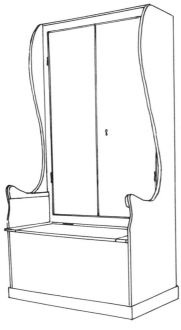

Armchair and bacon cupboard

became a 'carver chair' in the mid-19th century (not to be confused with the Carver chair of America), which is dealt with later in this section. The term elbow chair was then used for smaller armchairs around the house.

Country examples of all-wood combined armchair and bacon cupboard, with the cupboard opening either at the back, or in the front as in the example illustrated, had wings and curved arms and were the ancestors of upholstered wing chairs (see figure).

Astley-Cooper chair
See *Children's furniture*

Back-stool This was the earliest single chair without arms, which developed from the stool (see *Stool*). When life became comparatively more peaceful during the 16th century, with communal living in a hall no longer so customary, tables could be placed permanently in the middle of a room set aside specifically for dining. Seating would be placed all round the table, instead of against the wall, and people found themselves balancing on unsupported stools and benches. It soon became necessary to have some support for one's back other than the wall, and the legs at the rear of the stool were extended upwards to form the first single chair or – as it was then called – a 'back-stool'. These were in common use by the middle of the 17th century, when the back legs were also splayed to give greater stability. Stretchers were used to give added strength to the construction but as the 17th century proceeded the stretchers were moved upwards from their early position on the ground until they were halfway up the legs.

Early examples of back-stools (see figure) had flat seats with the frame sometimes a little higher than the seat itself to take a cushion, but with the extra well-upholstered clothing of the time this was not always necessary.

From a varied assortment of medieval spellings, however, we know that loose cushions (sometimes spelt quisshens, quisshyns, quishons and cusshyns) had probably always been used with stools. These were made of leather or woven fabric and stuffed with feathers, down or hair. Some chairs had holes in the seat to hold ropes upon which a cushion was supported.

From the time of the Commonwealth in the mid-17th century the term 'chair', 'single chair' or 'side chair' was usual instead of back-stool to distinguish this type from armchairs. In Essex inventories of the late 17th century there is no mention of the term back-stool, although it is still found occasionally in 18th century inventories.

Balloon-back chair In the context of country furniture, this term was applied to a common form of oval back chair with a cane seat, made in beech and birch, a large number of which were made from 1820 onwards, particularly in the High Wycombe district. It is of slender construction with an oval or balloon shaped back, with a single cross rail. Sometimes the oval is shaped into two letter Cs facing each other (see figure) to give the name 'Double C Ballon-back'; or with a rise in the oval of the back giving the name 'Camel-back', or with a dip in the oval which became known as the 'Rise and Fall'. The legs were tapered and splayed in Regency fashion. These chairs were often sold as 'Wycombe Whites' ready to be polished and painted. Often they were painted to resemble rosewood or with floral patterns added.

Banister-back chair
See *Restoration chair*, later in this section

Beehive chair
See *Basketry*

Bobbin-back chair
See *Spindle-back chair*, later in this section

Brewster chair This 17th century New England chair takes its modern name from William Brewster, an early leader of the

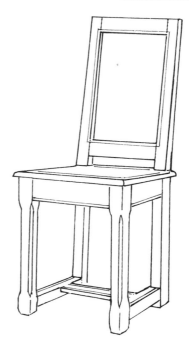

Back-stool (early 17th century)

'Double C' balloon back chair (*c.*1860)

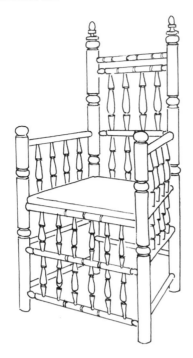

Brewster chair (New England; 17th century)

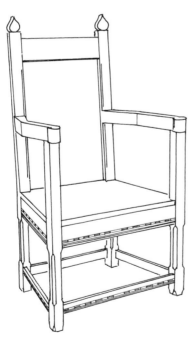

Salisbury caquetoire (late 17th century)

Massachusetts Bay Colony, who owned a chair of this type. The Brewster chair is a spindle-back or bobbin-back chair like the Carver chair described later in this section; it has double rows of spindles across the back, two rows down the sides under the armrests, one row above the seat and one below, and two rows of spindles under the front seat (see figure). It is usually made of ash or maple and often has a rush seat.

Cane chair

See *Caner; Restoration chair*, later in this section

Caquetoire This is the name given to a type of 16th century armchair with open canted arms, a tall narrow back and a shaped seat wider at the front than the back. It was a stage in the evolution of a lighter type of chair to the panel-back (see *Armchair*, earlier in this section).

In the Victoria and Albert Museum in London is a chair of this type dated about 1540 which was first discovered in a village in Devon. This has characteristic West Country carving on the back; but the chair has been found all over England. The name caquetoire comes from French chairs of this type and is derived from the verb 'caqueter', meaning to chatter, presumably because of the use made of it for gossiping.

Similar chairs were produced in Scotland at this time, due to the close alliance of the French and Scottish crowns. A fine Scottish chair in oak *c.* 1600 is illustrated (see photograph) which is similar to many French models of the late 16th century. The crest is of French inspiration, while the back has lunette carving on the panels, and palmated rails (see *Lunette, Palmated*).

Victor Chinnery, the author of *The Oak Tradition* has discovered as many as 22 chairs of caquetoire type in and around the Salisbury area of Wiltshire. Salisbury built its wealth on the wool trade with Europe and its close connections with the continent may well have introduced the style to the area. While some of

Scottish caquetoire (c.1600)

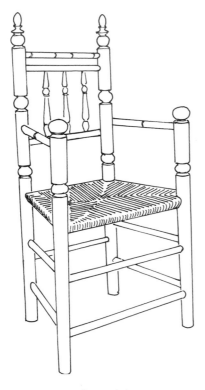

Carver chair
(New England, 17th century)

Chair-table
(early 17th century)

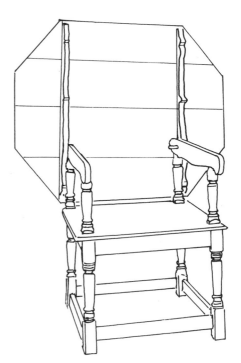

the Salisbury chairs have elaborate cresting, most have a lunette crest and some merely a carved top rail. The back panels vary from elaborate decoration to simple lozenge carving (see *Lozenge*). A plain example from a rustic workshop is illustrated (see figure, page 52). It is of late 17th century date, oak, with a plain elm panel. It has the canted arms of the Salisbury chairs, while the Scottish chairs have incurving arms. Another constructional detail in which the chairs differ is that the Scottish and French chairs have their arms joined to the back uprights both at the front and the sides, while the Salisbury chairs have their arms joined only to the front of the uprights.

Carver chair This is a 17th century New England chair. It takes its modern name from a chair of this type owned by John Carver, one of the Pilgrim Fathers, an Englishman from Nottingham who founded and became the first governor of the Plymouth colony in 1620. It is a spindle-back or bobbin-back chair with a

American chair-table with drawer
Old Sturbridge Village, Massachusetts

rush seat (see figure). The turned back legs extend upwards to form the back uprights topped with turned finials, and the front legs extend upwards to form supports for the arms. The top back rail is turned, and there are usually two horizontal rails in the back, joined by three vertical spindles. Hickory, maple and ash were favourite woods for these chairs.

The term 'carver' was also used in the 19th century to distinguish the armchair in a set of dining chairs from the single chairs.

Chair-table This dual purpose piece was very popular throughout the 16th century and

in the 17th century on both sides of the Atlantic. It was made by a joiner and had a back fitted with two rails hinged to the arms by pins. This back swung over and formed a table top, resting on the arms of the chair. The top could be secured by wooden pins inserted through the arm-rests.

The term 'monk's seat' is a modern term often incorrectly applied to these items.

The illustrations show a chair-table in the open and closed position of the top (see figures) and an American example, from Old Sturbridge Village, Massachusetts, has a drawer under the seat (see photograph).

Children's chairs
See *Children's furniture*

Close-chair (close-stool or commode chair)
Close-chairs are usually identified by the deep wooden apron below the seat, which hid the pewter or pottery chamber pot standing on the shelf beneath the hole in the seat, which was covered by a lid. They were made in considerable quantities in the fashionable woods and style of walnut and mahogany, as well as in oak and country woods in rural areas, and were in use in town and country before the invention of water closets.

While the chairs had backs and arms, the close-stool was in the form of an enclosed box, sometimes called a 'necessary stool'.

The term 'commode' used in Victorian times for these close-chairs earlier had a different meaning. It was used in the 18th century to mean a chest of drawers, often with a serpentine or semi-circular front.

Cockfighting chair This name has been wrongly attached to the type of reading and library chair where the occupant sits astride the chair, facing the back, which has a support for a book, resting his arms on wide arm rests at the sides. There is an 18th century picture of a cockfight which shows the man in charge sitting astride such a chair, which has given this type of chair its modern name (see figure).

Corner chair This type of chair was also known as a writing chair and as an elbow chair, and in America as a roundabout chair. It was popular in the 18th century and was made with a square wooden seat or rush seat, with a back

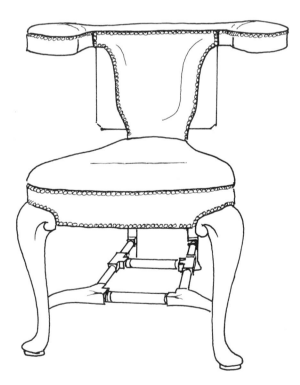

'Cockfighting' (correctly library or writing) chair
(18th century)

Country barber's chair (18th century)

Ladder-back corner chair (18th century)

on two sides of it. The oak chair illustrated (see figure) has a two-tier back with Chippendale type splats and is a type often used as a country barber's chair, the top acting as a headrest.

The rush-seated corner chair illustrated (see figure) has ladder-back type rails and a curved bow-shaped back and arm rail. This type of chair was the forerunner of the later low-back Windsor chair of the 19th century, such as the 'smoker's bow' which has a similar back rail (see *Windsor chair* later in this section). Cross-stretchers used in an X-formation are often found in later examples of corner chairs.

Country Chippendale chairs These are chairs made by country craftsmen after the publication of Thomas Chippendale's book of furniture designs, *The Gentleman and Cabinet Maker's Director*, in 1754. The book sold all over the country to cabinet-makers, carvers, joiners and upholsterers.

Chippendale (1718–1779) was born at Otley in Yorkshire, where his father was the village joiner and his grandfather a carpenter. He was established in London by 1748 and worked in St Martin's Lane, the famous 18th century centre for furniture, by 1753.

The country chairmakers made many chairs based on his designs in oak, beech and elm, which were made in mahogany in towns. They simplified and adapted these designs, for the most part keeping the seats of solid wood and giving their 'Chippendale style' touches to the rails and splats.

The armchair illustrated (see figure overleaf) has a splat in the Chippendale style of interlacing straps and scrolls.

The designs were not easy to carve in oak, but many examples were made. Often the chairs were made in several different woods for the various parts. When made in beech and oak they were sometimes stained to resemble

CHAIR *Country Chippendale chairs*

Chippendale style
armchair (1760)

Elm Chippendale style
side chair (1760)

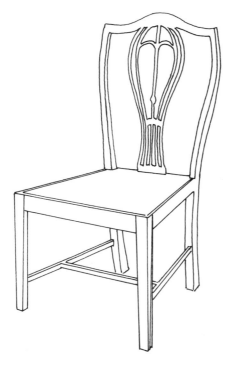

Oak Hepplewhite style chair
(late 18th century)

58

mahogany. The elm chairs were particularly attractive. The side chair illustrated (see figure) is in elm with a heart carved in the splat; this feature was often found in country chairs, perhaps indicating that they were made or bought on marriage.

Country Hepplewhite chairs This term is applied to the country craftsman's interpretation of the designs from the pattern book of George Hepplewhite. He was a cabinetmaker whose book *The Cabinet-maker and Upholsterer's Guide* was published in 1788, two years after his death. He interpreted many of the ideas of Robert Adam (1728–92) and some of the chairs made in these styles are also given the name 'Country Adam'. Adam was responsible for the classical revival of the late 18th century. The shield-back chairs of Hepplewhite's designs reflect this.

Later examples incorporated the Prince of Wales feathers design in the splat. The country chair illustrated shows how the craftsman has used these two ideas in an oak chair (see figure). The design is not easy to carry out in oak but he has given the top rail the shield-back shape and has used the Prince of Wales feather design in the splat.

Country Sheraton chairs These are chairs made by country craftsmen with features popularized by Thomas Sheraton (1751–1806) who came from Stockton-on-Tees in County Durham. When established in London, Sheraton published his drawing book of designs in 1791–4, which as in the case of Chippendale's book circulated all over the country, its aim being to acquaint cabinet-makers with the most up-to-date designs.

He illustrated a light, delicate type of furniture which was not altogether suited to country life. Much of the style of his painted chairs, however, with their lower backs, straight back rails and scroll-backs influenced country chairmakers, who later produced the scroll-back Windsors of the 19th century, and

the Mendlesham chairs of Suffolk (see *Windsor chair* and *Mendlesham chair*, later in this section).

Courting chair
See *Love seat*, later in this section

Cromwellian chair (or Commonwealth chair)
The chair usually associated with the austere Commonwealth period in England (1649–60) is the leather-covered single chair, decorated with brass nails, with turned legs and stretchers. The leather was stretched across the back and seat frames and nailed down without any stuffing being used. It was a development of the upholstered 16th century *Farthingale chair* (see overleaf). The chair continued to be made after the Cromwellian period which gave it its name, later with added straw stuffing for comfort. It was also found in the wealthier New England homes in the 17th and 18th centuries in which the leather side chairs were almost identical to the English types. It was found again in the Spanish colonies of California and New Mexico where leather work was especially loved and used (see photograph, page 61).

The chair was revived in the 19th century when it was called a 'Cromwell' chair.

The brass nails and the turning were the only form of decoration looked on with favour by the Puritans, and carving was little used on 17th century chairs until after the Restoration period in 1660, except in the earlier 'Yorkshire' types made in the north (see *Yorkshire chair* later in this section).

The brass nails were permitted as they were functional, not merely decorative, and turning was a type of decoration derived naturally from the skill of the turner and so was quite acceptable. Bobbin turning, the simplest of types, was used for legs and stretchers. Where the stretchers joined the legs the turning was omitted and the legs and stretchers left square to give the joints greater strength. Applied

Plain Cromwellian chair of a type found
in farmhouses (*c.* 1660)

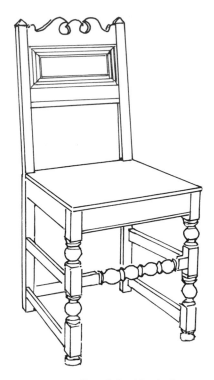

Cromwellian chair with raised
back panel (*c.*1660)

decoration in the form of split spindles was
glued to the uprights to take the place of the
carving that was now frowned upon.

The lack of decoration other than turning
restored the attention to the wood used and the
design of the chair that was to become so
significant in the 18th century.

A plain chair of the Cromwellian period is
illustrated (see figure), probably more usual in
farmhouses than the leather variety.

Many all-wood chairs of the second half of
the 17th century followed the trend to lighter
chairs by having the back-panel raised clear of
the seat, giving a gap of varying size (see
figure).

Derbyshire chair
See *Yorkshire chair*, later in this section

Elbow chair
See *Corner chair*, later in this section

Farthingale chair This was an extra wide
back-stool (see *Back-stool*, earlier in this
section) made in the late 16th and 17th
centuries to accommodate the large hooped
farthingale skirts of the ladies of fashion. It was
given this name in Victorian times. The chair
was made in large numbers by upholsterers
and had its seat and back made of a framework
of beech, covered by fabric. It is doubtful
whether country ladies had either the skirts or
the time to need such a chair; the all-wood
varieties of back-stools were more probably
seen in the country (see figure overleaf).

Glastonbury chair This is a type of wooden
folding stool made in the 16th century, its arms
hinged by a wooden rod through the side rails
of the seat and upper part of the legs in front.
The name is believed to stem from a drawing of
such a chair in Henry Shaw's *Specimens of*

Cromwellian chair: brass nails and turning were the only form of decoration approved by the Puritans; this style of chair was found both sides of the Atlantic. *Victoria and Albert Museum*

Farthingale chair (*c.*1684)

Ancient Furniture, published in 1836 (so the name is comparatively modern), which was described as the abbot's chair, Glastonbury. Such chairs are often found in the chancels of country churches.

Great chair
See *Armchair*, earlier in this section

Ladder-back chair This is a modern term for a large number of country chairs which developed in the north of England in the 17th century from the earlier 'Yorkshire' type chairs (see *Yorkshire chair*), which had horizontal rails linking the back uprights. They were made in elm, oak and beech and were usually rush-seated. The ladder rails were framed into the back uprights and were found in a large variety of shapes throughout the 18th and 19th centuries. The chair also appeared in armchair and rocking chair forms. Two 18th century

ladder-back chairs are illustrated (see figures).

The ladder-back was a country style that eventually found its way to the 18th century cabinet makers in towns. It was popular especially in the period 1740–90, and was made in mahogany, often with the ladder rails pierced.

Like the spindle-back chair it was revived by the Cotswold school of furniture makers, in designs by Ernest Gimson (see figure) inspired by William Morris in the early 20th century (see *Cotswold school; William Morris*).

The ladder-back chair could be found in the 17th century New England colonies, where it is called a slat-back or banister-back, becoming very popular in the early 18th century. The chairs were made in hickory and maple woods with rush seats, and were of sturdier construction than the English chairs. The horizontal slats were wider, with three to six slats, again in a variety of shapes. The front legs were extended to form arm supports, as in the spindle-back, and were often topped with large mushroom-shaped finials (see photograph overleaf). The back legs extended to form the back uprights and were topped with ornamental finials, often lemon-shaped. Types of slat-backs from Pennsylvania were plainer. As in the case of the English ladder-backs, the American chairs were revived again in the 19th century, in their case by the Shakers (see *Shaker furniture*).

Lancashire chair
See *Yorkshire* and *Spindle-back chairs*, later in this section

Leather chairs
See *Cromwellian chair*, earlier in this section

Love seat
Modern term for a double armchair with a seat large enough to accommodate two persons. These are found in oak with panelled arms backs and open arms. They were especially popular in Wales.

The term 'courting chair' was also used.

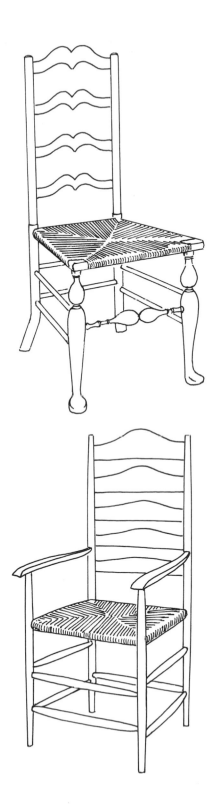

Rush-seated
ladder-back chair
(18th century)

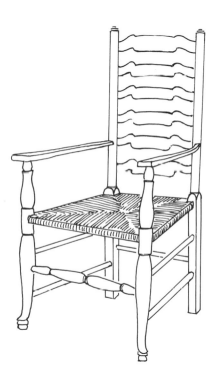

Another type of
rush-seated ladder-back
(18th century)

Ladder-back chair
in the Ernest Gimson style
(early 20th century)

Mortuary chair
See *Yorkshire chair*, later in this section

Nursing chairs Low forms of most types of country chairs have been made for the use of mothers while nursing their babies, the rocking chair being an especially popular type for this purpose. Many full-size chairs are found with the legs cut down for use as nursing chairs, but chairs specially made for nursing have lowers arms than ordinary armchairs.

A nursing chair in High Wycombe Museum in Buckinghamshire is fan-back Windsor (see under *Windsor chair*), with the comb cut from a wide section of timber and sawn and shaped into a curve which follows the line of the seat, the sticks in the back repeating this curve to fit around the body of the chair snugly. This type of chair is sometimes called a 'shawl-back', probably because a shawl draped over the comb would make a draughtproof alcove. A nursing chair was known in America as a slipper chair.

Panel-back chairs
See *Armchair*, earlier in this section

'Queen Anne' (or Curvilinear) chair The graceful lines of legs and backs of chairs in the 'Queen Anne' period (1700–1725) influenced country chairmakers in the early part of the 18th century. They produced a modified version of the back which had a curved cresting of the top rail reminiscent of a milkmaid's yoke, which in fact was called a yoke rail even in fashionable circles. The oak chair illustrated (see figure) from the early 18th century is a transitional style where the turned legs and uprights are of the William and Mary period, but the country craftsman has used the fiddle shaped splat of the Queen Anne period in the back. A plain splat was used as oak did not lend itself to the elaborate carving possible in walnut and mahogany. Early splats were at first framed to the cresting and bottom rail, and later to the seat.

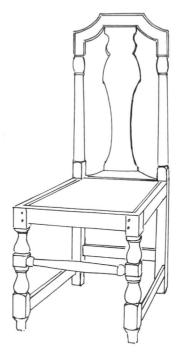

'Queen Anne' style oak chair
(early 18th century)

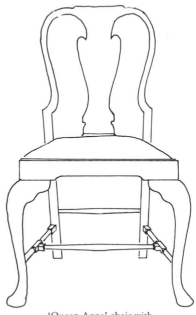

'Queen Anne' chair with
cabriole legs and stretchers
(18th century)

65

New England ladder-back (17th century)
American Museum in Britain, Bath

Slat-backed chair (*c.*1680)

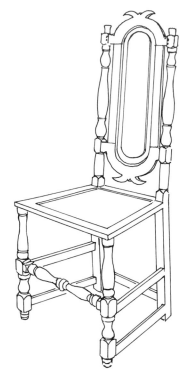

Oak chair with arched cresting
(Welsh; late 17th century)

Country chairs had cane or rush instead of upholstered seats long after these became obsolete in towns.

A later farmhouse chair (see figure, page 65) in walnut has a similar splat but this time the country craftsman has attempted the cabriole leg of the period, linking it with stretchers still in use in the countryside.

One reason country chairmakers were not fond of too many curves in backs and cabriole legs was that these forms used a great deal of wood to produce the curves in one piece, and they preferred more economical styles.

Restoration chair The restoration of Charles II to the throne of England in 1660 is a dividing line between the furniture produced by carpenters, joiners and turners up to this date and the fashionable furniture produced by cabinet makers in the second half of the 17th

century. The latter were influenced by the craftsmen of France and Holland who had been entering England in increasing numbers, and also the court of the restored King who had spent so much time on the Continent. While town fashions moved quickly ahead from this point, introducing new imported woods and new methods of construction to the great furniture designers of the 18th century, country craftsmen continued to produce the well-tried designs of the previous centuries, which they would make throughout the next century.

However, gradually the trend to lighter types of chairs reached country workshops and by the end of the 17th century they were producing their own versions of the fashionable, highly-carved tall chairs which were made in walnut with cane seats and backs associated with the Charles II period.

In place of the cane, which was not easily obtainable, they made harder-wearing rush seats. In place of the elaborate carving they used simple turning in beech, elm and yew instead of walnut. They devised the *slat-backed chair* to give a similar effect to cane, using wooden slats, which was stronger for country use (see figure).

In America the slat-back chair was also called a *banister-back* and could be seen in 18th century New England living rooms, made in maple which was often stained to look like ebony, and with split banisters in the back. This rural chair, widely used in America, also had turned supports topped with tall finials and a crested and carved top back rail.

The solid back panel of earlier chairs was separated from the stiles and joined to the top rail and bottom rail in chairs of the second half of the 17th century. This is shown in the late 17th century oak chair from Wales with an arched cresting, turned supports and a fielded back panel (see figure).

This separated back panel, made in cane in town chairs, in the 18th century became the slender, fiddle-shaped splat of the Queen Anne period. In each stage of its development the chair became lighter and more movable, but in country examples always remained sturdy.

Rocking chair This chair with curved rocking slats connecting the back and front legs developed concurrently in England and America in the latter part of the 18th century. It was in the 19th century, however, that it became popular and even then its acceptance in

Rocking chair
(English; 19th century)
Museum of English Rural Life,
Reading

'Boston rocker' (19th century)
American Museum in Britain, Bath

England was much slower than in America, where it soon became a firm favourite. The Victorians never quite took to their rocking chairs and for a long time only approved them 'on medical grounds'.

In England even in the late 19th century the rocking chair was simply a chair of an existing type to which rockers had been added (see photograph). While this was done to rush-seated ladder-backs, spindle-backs and Windsor chairs of all kinds, only in America with the development of the Boston Rocker did a chair specially designed for rocking and for comfort appear and remain a standard type. American rocking chairs are often found made in as many as four different woods in one chair, such as oak legs, walnut rockers, hickory spindles and the seat and back of maple.

Boston Rocker

This is an American 19th century rocking chair with a roll seat, deeply curving upwards, curved arms and a wide top rail which was usually decorated with painted stencilled designs. The back and arms have delicate spindles (see photograph).

Salem rocker

A 19th century rocking chair made in New England with a lower back than the Boston rocker, and with a heavily scrolled seat and arms.

Shaker rocker

See *Shaker furniture*

Windsor rocking chairs

These were made on both sides of the Atlantic, but in England no special design for rocking was made. It was quite common in High Wycombe workshops for a range of rockers to be held which could be quickly fitted to any style of Windsor chair the customer required. In America the arrow-back was widely made as a rocking chair. A type with an added comb above the top rail is shown (see figure); this

Arrow-back rocking chair with comb
(American; early 18th century)

was much more common in America than in England.

Roundabout chair
See Corner chair, earlier in this section

Slipper chair
See *Nursing chair*, earlier in this section

Slat-back chair
See *Ladder-back chairs; Restoration chairs*, earlier in this section

Spindle-back chairs Also described as 'bobbin-back', these chairs developed in the north of England where turned chairs had always been popular; they are often called Lancashire chairs. They were eventually produced all over the country and found in almost every farmhouse. Early 17th century chairs had thick upright posts forming legs and

Sausage turned spindle-back chair
(New Jersey; late 17th or early 18th century)
American Museum in Britain, Bath

Spindle-back chair (19th century)

Spindle-back rocking chair (19th century)

back posts in one, and front legs continuing upwards to form supports for the arms. The chair is seen in this form in America in the early New England Carver and Brewster chairs. The 17th century chair illustrated (see photograph) from the American Museum at Bath is of late 17th or early 18th century date and comes from New Jersey. It has a form of sausage turning in the back, and is made of red mulberry wood.

In the 18th century single, rocking and armchairs were produced, principally in the north of England at first, which had slender, vertical turned spindles between two or three horizontal rails in the back. They were often in beechwood and with rush seats. The styles changed little through the years, and it is often difficult to tell if a chair is of 18th or 19th century date (see figure).

The 19th century rocking chair shown here

(see figure) comes from Lancaster Museum.

The spindle-back style was revived again in this century by the Cotswold school of designers inspired by William Morris. A yew chair with bobbin turnings in the back and a rush seat is shown (see photograph overleaf), designed by Ernest Gimson and made at Daneway House Workshops, Sapperton. (See also *Carver chair, Brewster* and *Turned chairs*, in this section.)

Table-chair
See *Chair-table*

Thrown chair
See Turned chair, below

Triangular chair
See *Turned chair*, below

Bobbin-turned spindle-back chair
designed by Ernest Gimson (20th century)
Victoria and Albert Museum

Turned chair (Welsh; *c.*1550)
National Museum of Wales

Turned chair This was often called a 'thrown chair' ('thrown' being a woodworker's term meaning having been turned on a lathe) and was a development of the triangular stool with turned legs. It was made by turners from medieval times.

The turners made a wide variety of turned parts for arms, backs and legs; these were socketed into the seat, which was often triangular. This construction eventually led in the early 18th century to the simpler and more elegant designs of the Windsor chair. The patterns of these early turned chairs became very complex by the 16th century, highly decorative in a frenzied kind of way, but not very comfortable. They were not unnaturally also known as 'turned-all-over' chairs. Ash was a favourite wood for these over-ambitious examples of the turner's art, the more ornate examples coming from the Severn valley, Wales, Cheshire and Lancashire. A great variety of woods were used, however, the turner using whatever tree was near at hand. It was in these counties that the spindle-back chairs developed in the 18th century.

The example of the turner's art from Wales illustrated here is of about 1550 date, and is in oak with a square seat (see photograph).
(See also *Spindle-back*, earlier in this section.)

Upholstered chairs While few upholstered chairs would have found their way into farmhouses and cottages, the farthingale chairs of the 16th century had upholstered seats, as also did some armchairs in the 17th century. These are often mentioned in inventories as being covered with 'Turkey work'. This was a textile, the technique of which was imitated from imported Turkish carpets. The flowers decorating it are similar to contemporary English embroidery.
(See also *Cofferer*.)

Wainscot chair This was an alternative name given to oak armchairs until the 17th century. (See also *Armchair*, earlier in this section.)

WINDSOR CHAIR

A Windsor chair is one in which the legs, arm supports, back stays and sticks are all socketed directly into round holes in the seat itself. The seat is usually saddle shaped, though it can be circular and is cut from a single plank. It is a chair with 250 years of history on both sides of the Atlantic.

Various explanations for the name have been put forward, the most likely being the fact that the largest area for their production in the 18th century was in the High Wycombe district of Buckinghamshire. From here large quantities of both completed chairs and parts for assembly went to the nearby Windsor market *en route* for London. In Somerset chairs of the Windsor type have always been known as 'stickbacks', and probably this was the name given to all the early Windsors, the name Windsor only being attached to them when they were brought to the notice of fashionable London.

That they were known as Windsor chairs in America as early as 1708 is demonstrated by an inventory of that date of the goods of a Philadelphia merchant, John Jones, which includes three Windsor chairs. This inventory is mentioned in *The Furniture of our Forefathers* (1900) by Esther Singleton. Whether these particular chairs were taken to America from England or whether made in America is not known. This is again the case where five Windsor chairs are included among the goods of Governor Patrick Gordon, who died in 1736, having arrived in Philadelphia in 1726. If Windsor chairs were imported by the American colonists, they were obviously soon copied as they were cheap and easy to produce.

The Windsor chair was first mentioned in England in writing by Lord Percival in 1724; it occurs again in a catalogue of 1728 and an advertisement of 1730.

An early example of a low-back Windsor chair came from Cardiganshire in Wales and is of a type that has long been known in Welsh farmhouses. It is easy to see how such a chair

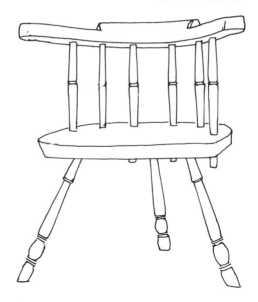

Elm and birch low-back Windsor chair
(Welsh; late 18th century)

could have developed from the universally used three-legged stool, as did the elaborate chairs made by turners. These Cardiganshire chairs, found in the west and north-west of Wales, have thick plank seats of elm or bog oak, with a semi-circular back supported by birch or beech spindles, and three legs for better balance on uneven floors. The late 18th century example illustrated (see figure) has a seat and back of elm and legs of birch. A similar chair is in St Cross Hospital near Winchester and has been assigned dates ranging from the 14th to 16th centuries. The legs of the early examples were roughly shaped with an axe and a draw-knife.

That chairs of these types had been made in country districts for many years by local carpenters and turners is probably the reason that the Windsor chair emerged at the turn of the 18th century, as Ivan Sparkes says, as a fully developed style 'without the usual trail of crude or early examples littering the path of its development'. The high standard that turning had achieved over the years made this possible.

Early assembly-line production The popularity of the Windsor chair grew apace due to the fact that it was simple to produce and economic in the use of materials. It has always lent itself to assembly-line production, and in England it was usual for the various parts to be produced by different craftsmen, even in small workshops or factories that employed perhaps half a dozen men. The legs and stretchers were made by turners, often bodgers working in local woodland, the seat was shaped by a bottomer with an adze, sawn parts were provided by a benchman in the workshop, the bows and curved parts were steamed and bent by a bender, and the whole chair was assembled by the framer; he often also stained and finished the chair, unless it was to be sold 'in the white'. The latter types were often left like this and kept clean by scouring with sand.

In some smaller factories one of these craftsmen might be responsible for more than one process, but the same basic division into benchman and framer has continued to this day.

Few craftsmen were able to make a Windsor chair from start to finish. One of the last was H. E. (Jack) Goodchild who in his Naphill workshop combined the tasks of bodger, benchman and framer to produce chairs of outstanding quality and workmanship (see figure). He died in 1950.

Occasionally Windsor chairs were signed by the benchman putting initials and a pattern number on the back edge of the seat. These are sometimes identifiable in the records of chairmaking factories or in old directories.

The situation was different in America where all the stages in the making of a Windsor chair would be carried out by one man with the aid of one or two journeymen and apprentices.

Chippendale style Windsor chair

The names of many early American craftsmen are known, from 1740 onwards.

Two 18th century craftsmen from High Wycombe whose names we do know are Samuel Treacher and Thomas Widgington. The latter is believed to have established the first actual chairmaking factory in High Wycombe about 1810.

By 1875 it is believed that 4,700 chairs a day were being made in the Wycombe area, so that when mechanization came, the industry lent itself to factory production without difficulty. The origins of mass production in the furniture industry started with the making of Windsor chairs. These continue to be made up to the present day by firms whose founders were among the earliest names in the production of Windsor chairs.

Although the High Wycombe area has always been the most famous for this production, the beech forest of Buckinghamshire providing both the wood and the working area for the bodgers, Windsor chairs were also made in Berkshire, Lancashire, Nottinghamshire, Yorkshire, Norfolk, Suffolk, North Wales, Somerset, Devon, Cornwall and London. A small colony of Windsor chairmakers worked in the Rockley area of Nottinghamshire between 1825–1865. Here it was the wood from Sherwood Forest that was used. About fifty chairs from this district have been located bearing the impressed mark of 'F Walker/Rockley'.

The Windsor chair's growth in America Windsor chairmaking was a recognized trade in the New England colonies of America by 1770. The furniture trade was centred in Philadelphia at the beginning of the 18th century, and this became one of the most important centres for the production of Windsor chairs, producing the low-back Windsors, which were later also made in New Jersey and New York. The *Philadelphia low-back* was in production by about 1725.

The earliest Windsors were of the *comb-back*

variety. They were made from 1700–1800, and from 1830–1900 in a heavier design; in America from 1740–1780 (see photograph overleaf).

The Windsor chair in America differed from its English counterpart in that right from its beginning it was accepted as a welcome piece of furniture in all classes of homes. In England it was a favourite in farmhouses and cottages, useful in pleasure gardens, parks, public buildings, taverns and coffee houses and the servants' quarters of great houses. It was only rarely found in more wealthy living rooms. In America, as well as fulfilling its public duties the Windsor chair was accepted in the homes of the highest in the land, so that from about 1750 onwards it developed in its own way from the early comb-backs to a wide variety of light and graceful styles. The *New England bow-back* armchair shows a feature common in America but seldom found in England, of the use of the comb with the bow to heighten the back of the chair forming a comfortable headrest.

Local woods The variety of Windsors was also influenced on both sides of the Atlantic by the local woods used by village craftsmen. The woods used in America included pine, chestnut, maple, oak, hickory and ash. Pine and chestnut were favoured for seats instead of the elm used in England; maple was used for legs, arms and stretchers, also for arrow-backs and hickory for spindles and bows as it did not fracture when steamed and bent.

The English craftsmen used beech, especially for the bent parts, also ash, willow, yew, oak, walnut, cherry and other fruitwoods. Where different fruitwoods were used for the various parts the craftsman relied on staining, painting and polishing to 'match up' the chair. Painted Windsors were found in black, green, red or yellow, the latter being a favourite colour for children's chairs. Indian red was a colour often used in America.

Developing styles The history of the Windsor chair in England in the 18th century mirrors the development in town furniture. The ornamental splats never found in American chairs are a help in dating the English chairs, although plain splats were popular throughout the century. Cabriole legs, Gothic arches and cowhorn stretchers appeared in England, particularly in the *bow-back* designs that developed from the earlier *comb-backs*. The ornamental splats that appear in these chairs in such a great variety helped to prolong the popularity of the English bow-back, particularly the *wheel-back* style. These splats were cut from patterns made of paper or wood, often several at a time clamped in a vice. A hole was bored for each part of the design and a small blade of a bow saw or keyhole saw inserted to cut out each shape.

The *fan-back* Windsor was popular on both sides of the Atlantic, but the Americans developed the style to include many graceful variations. American chairs are only called fan-backs if the sticks at the back rise from the seat without an arm-bow crossing the back.

The wheel-back chair ended the development of the traditional Windsor chair in England about 1820. Two types of country chairs were developed from the Windsor chair from about this date, the *scroll-back* and the *lath-back*. The scroll-back had strong links with the styles of the Regency period, as did the *rod-back* chairs in America. All types of Windsor chairs were made in the 19th century as single chairs, armchairs, rocking chairs and children's chairs. *Low-back* Windsors were made in the 19th century also with the arms and yoke rail following a continuous line, revivals of the 18th century *Philadelphia low-back*. These appeared as the *smoker's bow* and the *berger bow* in England and the *firehouse Windsor* and the *Captain's chair* in America. 19th century Windsors also appeared with both solid and caned seats, as commodes and even as swivel chairs. Plain wooden seated armchairs were made throughout the 19th century at High Wycombe, some low-back and some of

a heavy looking ladder-back construction.

Loudon writing in 1833 said the Windsor chair was one of the best kitchen chairs in general use in the Midlands.

When William Morris was looking for chairs to furnish the premises for his new Socialist League and wanted chairs which reflected his views on the return to furniture that was at the same time beautiful, simple and useful, he chose Windsor chairs. His firm, Morris & Co. was producing a type of Windsor chair based on a traditional Sussex design in 1865 (see photograph overleaf). (See also *Benchman; Bender; Bodger; Framer.*)

Arch-back 1765–80 American
This was an elaboration of the loop-back where the back bow, after being steamed as usual, was clamped into a specially made frame to shape the back and arms in one piece. It was chiefly made in New England. Much skill in bending the back bow was needed to make this shape. The chair illustrated (see figure overleaf) has a braced back.

Chairs of this type 'made in England' have also been identified in Devon by Gabriel Olive. A stick-back chair industry was established at Yealmpton, near Plymouth in the 19th century. The arch-back chairs made there have their spindles secured at the top with small square oak pins driven through the bow from the front. They were also made with braced backs. It is possible that an American or American-trained craftsman settled in Yealmpton and founded the industry there.

Arrow-back c. 1810–35 American
A development of the rod-back chair, the back having a strong backward sweep and the arms shaped in a cyma-curve (see *Cyma curve*). The flat arrow-shaped splats in the back were often of maple wood. The legs and stretchers are of the box type and bamboo ringed. This was one of the first Windsors to appear as a rocking chair; also found as a writing armchair.

76

Comb-back Windsor chair
Museum of English Rural Life, Reading

Chair made by William Morris & Co inspired by the traditional
Sussex Windsor chair   *Victoria and Albert Museum*

Arch-back Windsor chair (New England; 1765–80)　　　Wheel-back Windsor chair (late 18th century)

Bow-back (Hoop-back) 18th and 19th centuries
This chair developed from the comb-back
about 1740. The comb piece was replaced by a
bent bow, giving a back with a double bow.
The chair was also made as a side chair with a
single bow, in a low-back style.

The bow-back was also called a sack-back,
loop-back or oval-back in America. While the
American chairs are usually more narrowly
waisted than the English, this is not always so,
and narrowly waisted bow-backs are seen in
many of the illustrations to the books of
Charles Dickens.

Bow-back chairs made in Yealmpton in
Devon have been identified by Gabriel Olive,
and these have American characteristics. They
normally have seven spindles, sometimes with
bamboo-style turnings, with alternate spindles
secured at the top with small square oak pins
driven through the bow from the front. Some
chairs have diagonal braces at the back. The

armchairs in the group have arms consisting of
a flat piece of ash, bent at right angles and
dowelled into the seat and bow, in the manner
of American loop-back armchairs of the years
1785–1810. The seats of the Devon chairs are
usually of elm, but sometimes of sycamore or
birch. The legs are fitted nearer to the centre of
the seat than is usual on English chairs, though
without as much splay as on American ones.

The American sack-back chairs were made
from 1750–1820. They were wider than the
English bow-backs and sometimes had an
abbreviated comb added as a headrest. They
never achieved the great popularity of the
English bow-backs, perhaps because they
were never made with the decorated back splat
introduced into the English versions in the
middle of the 18th century.

The wheel-back design (see figure) became
the most popular at the end of the century and
has been made ever since.

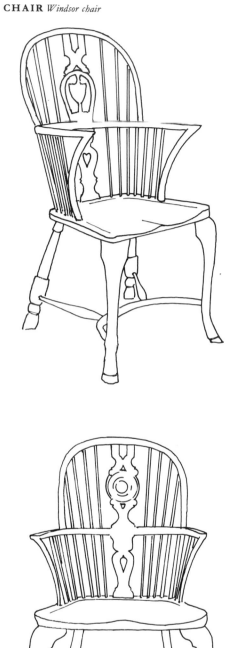

'Hepplewhite' Windsor
with classical urn motif
(late 18th to early
19th centuries)

Bow-back Windsor chair
with Prince of Wales feathers
motif (1810–1820)

Hepplewhite period
Windsor chair with disc
motif (1820–30)

Bow-back Windsor (early 19th century)

Chippendale Windsor with cabriole legs

Other splats had classical urn motifs or vase designs (see figure) in the late 18th to early 19th centuries.

Prince of Wales feathers were popular (see figure) in the Hepplewhite period and Regency period (1810–20).

A splat with a disc or turned wheel was used about 1820–30 and is illustrated in a chair made in yew (see figure). A cross and a six-rayed star are also found.

These chairs often had cabriole legs and the cowhorn stretchers which only appear in English designs. The cabriole leg was never a very happy addition to a Windsor chair design, but often attempted. Usually it only appears on the front legs, but occasionally all four legs are in cabriole style and appear with or without stretchers.

Early 19th century bow-back Windsors, influenced by plainer Sheraton styles show a return to a simple horse-shoe back without a splat and with turned legs (see figure).

But there is no doubt that the use of the decorated splats increased and prolonged the popularity of the bow-back designs in England.

Chippendale Windsor 1770–1800 English
This chair takes its name from the use of several features associated in chairs in the Chippendale *Director* of 1754, particularly in the use of pierced splats. It was made in both comb-back and bow-back styles and was popular in some districts until the middle of the 19th century. The Chippendale designs were of course simplified as in other versions of 'country Chippendale' chairs. Both the splats and the amount of piercing were usually reduced.

Early types of comb-back Windsor chair

This style often appeared with the cabriole leg and cow-horn stretcher, and was the style made by the last Chiltern chairmaker, Jack Goodchild, working in a cottage workshop by himself (see figure, previous page).

Comb-back Windsor 1700–1800, 1830–1900 England; 1740–1780 America
This Windsor has the back stands and sticks fixed into the seat at the bottom and socketed into a rail or comb at the top, giving the appearance of a wide-toothed comb. The length of the back sticks can be as much as three feet.

The earliest types (see figures) had plain stick legs, shaped with an axe and draw knife to a rounded shape, which were socketed into the seat, and no stretchers. Sometimes the seat was saddle-shaped and sometimes plain. Sometimes the back spindles tapered as each end; often they were plain.

The top back rail was originally elaborately shaped, a design carried over from the cresting rails of Restoration chairs. In America this feature was much exaggerated, the ears being extended, it has been suggested, to hang a small oil lamp for a light for reading and sewing. The ears at the ends of the comb were gently curved in the Goldsmith design and more deeply carved as rosettes in other examples.

Where the comb was narrower than the seat the chair was known as a balloon-back.

The Goldsmith chair takes its name from a Windsor comb-back, once owned by writer Oliver Goldsmith, (1730–74) now in the Victoria and Albert Museum. Chairs in this style have been produced to this day. The round seat has a bobtail extension cut out of the solid, with supporting diagonal brace sticks. The legs are sharply splayed outwards with a single H-stretcher. The comb is slightly wider than the seat giving the impression of a fan-back.

The design was introduced into America about 1770, and while American designers moved on to produce the graceful styles of the New England and Philadelphia comb-backs, the English reverted to the more stumpy varieties of Windsor chairs.

The Philadelphia comb-back has 5–9 spindles carried through the arm-bow to the comb, which stands about 15 inches above the arm-bow. The legs have blunt arrow turnings.

The New England comb-back produced from about 1740–80 has baluster turned legs set into the seat with a more angled rake than most comb-backs. The height can be as much as 107 cm (41 in) above the arm-bow. In late models the arm-bow loses its raised cresting

and develops into a plain slender unpretentious bow (see figure).

From 1740–1770 in England the back with a splat incorporated was usual, first a plain urn shape, combined with the cabriole legs of the Queen Anne period and turned stretchers (see figure). Plain splats continued to be made for many years in country areas, but pierced ornamental splats were also used, with Chippendale designs (see figure).

An early 19th century chair shows Sheraton's influence in the curved top rail, pierced splat and turned legs (see figure overleaf).

Fan-back Windsor
This is a comb-back Windsor dating from 1750 onwards, which has the comb widened to give a fan shape. Most of the English chairs rely heavily on the armbow which crosses the back of the chair for the strength of their con-

New-England comb-back Windsor chair
(Late 18th century)

Comb-back Windsor with urn-decorated splat
and cabriole legs (1740–1770)

Comb-back Windsor with pierced ornamented
splat (late 18th century)

Comb-back Windsor with curved top rail and
pierced splat (early 19th century)

Gothic Windsor chair (mid-18th century,
revived early 19th century)

Gothic Windsor chair (1760)

struction. In America a chair is only given this name if the back sticks rise unobstructed from the seat.

The chair was made as an armchair and a side chair and in the late 18th century with Chippendale splat and cabriole legs.

The New England fan-back was made from 1760–1800 and was popular both as a side chair and as an armchair. Some designs have the projecting bobtail at the back and bracing sticks, giving extra support and adding grace to the design. It generally has vase and ring turnings in the legs and back uprights (see *Vase turning*).

Gothic Windsor 1760–80 English
The bow-back came under the influence of the Gothic revival which took place in the middle of the 18th century. The sticks were replaced by one carved and pierced central splat, with a smaller splat on each side, which with the pointed Gothic back were all reminiscent of Gothic windows and archways. It also had cabriole legs (see figures). The style was revived in the early 19th century.

Lancashire and Yorkshire Windsor
This was a heavier type of Windsor with an elaborate splat in the back, and apart from the elm wood seat, it was generally made of all yew wood. It was made in many northern counties in the 19th century, including the Rockley area of Nottinghamshire, but it became a standard model in many other areas. It had heavily turned sausage stretchers, with triple rings and cup turnings on the legs (see figure).

Low-back Windsors

Berger bow c. 1840–65 English
An elaborately decorated form of the smoker's bow chair taking its name from the Bergère upholstered half-couch, popular at the time. It has a high curved back supported by spindles or banisters or a combination of both.

Lancashire Windsor chair (19th century)

Captain's chair 1875–1900 American
A low-back Windsor used in the pilot houses of boats on the Mississippi. The arms curve downwards and are socketed into the seat.

Firehouse Windsor 1850–1870 American
A low-back Windsor widely used in furnishing the quarters of American volunteer fire companies, also hotels and offices. It has a U-shaped seat and seven turned spindles in the back. The front legs are only slightly turned and the back legs are straight.

Mendlesham or 'Dan Day'
This is a type of low-back Windsor which appeared in the early 19th century. The chair originated in the village of Mendlesham in Suffolk, made by the local wheelwright and chairmaker, Daniel Day, but by 1830 and until

Low-back Windsor chair of Mendlesham
or Dan Day type (1830–1850)

1850 it was being produced by other makers as well.

The chair has a Sheraton style back rail with a square finish. The top back rail is a double rail with three turned balls between. This is joined to the bottom rail with a variety of spindles and splats. Fifteen examples of the chair can be seen in Ipswich Museum. Sometimes the small back sticks are plain, occasionally turned. The small ornamental splats have a variety of pierced designs. While the bottom rail can be plain and straight, it is more usually double, with two balls between the top and bottom parts, the lower often curved downwards (see figure). The chairs have turned legs with the decoration high up and are joined by H-stretchers. They were made in yew and fruitwood, with saddle-shaped seats of elm.

The chair was usually made as an armchair, but a rare set of four single chairs is in Ipswich Museum. These, like some of the other

Mendlesham or 'Dan Day' Windsor chairs, with bobtail extension and braced back   *Ipswich Museum*

Philadelphia low-back Windsor chair with
baluster turned legs (1725–1780)

Smoker's bow Windsor chair (1830 onwards)

Mendlesham chairs, have a bobtail extension
to the seat and a braced back (see photograph).

Philadelphia Low-back c. 1725–1780 American
This chair, like the 19th century English
Smoker's bow and Berger chairs, probably
originated from the writing chairs of the
Queen Anne period in the early 18th century,
which were popular at the time this chair came
into production in the mid-18th century. It has
a wide saddled U-shape seat and curved
armbow. The chair originated in Philadelphia,
but was also made in New Jersey and New
York 1750–1780, when the chair was given a
much higher cresting along the arm and
baluster turned legs (see figure).

Smoker's Bow 1830 onwards English
This low-back Windsor probably takes its
name from its great popularity in smoking
rooms, reading rooms, clubs and offices, inns
and cafés in the mid-19th century. The chair

was made with solid and with cane seats, and
was in use well into the 20th century. A version
decorated with splats instead of spindles was
made in High Wycombe during the 1880s. The
smoker's bow was revived after the second
World War and is again being produced.
Modern varieties have the height somewhat
reduced (see figure).

Rod-back c. 1800–1830 American
Like the Mendlesham chairs this has a
Sheraton influence in the straight back rail.
Unlike most American Windsors the legs have
very little flare outwards and are supported by
H-stretchers or box-stretchers. Many are
painted with decorations in the Sheraton style.
The example shown is an armchair with box-
stretcher and bamboo style turnings (see
photograph overleaf).

Scroll-back or stay-back 1860–1890 English
A Regency style Windsor chair without the
bow and sticks, the back having no comb. The

87

Rod-back-Windsor armchair with box stretcher and bamboo style turnings (American, 1800–1830)
American Museum in Britain, Bath

two back stands or uprights are 'scrolled over' or curled backwards at the top, just above the top rail (see figure).

A Gothic element is often introduced by arches cut into the stay across the back, supported by turned spindles acting as miniature pillars (see figure).

Large numbers of plain wooden seat scroll-backs were made from 1880–1890 (see figure).

A variation of the scroll-back was made by a Windsor chairmaker of Oxford about 1846–69. His name was Stephen Hazell and his chairs had Sheraton style arms curving downwards to the seat, and linked to it by a turned spindle. This type of chair was soon made by other manufacturers (see figure).

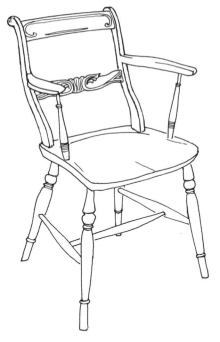

Scroll-back (or stay-back) Windsor chair
(1860–1890)

Gothic type scroll-back Windsor chair
(late 19th century)

Plain wood scroll-back Windsor chair
(1880–1890)

Variation of scroll-back type Windsor chair
by Stephen Hazell (Oxford; c.1860)

Writing chair 1760–1860 American
This was a design not produced in England and made in all types of Windsor chair design in America, many of the chairs probably to special orders. The example illustrated (see photograph) is a painted slat back with turned legs and stretchers from the American Museum at Bath. The oval-shaped writing surface has a drawer underneath. It is of 1780–90 date.

Thomas Jefferson composed the first draft of the 'Declaration of Independence' in America in 1776, while sitting in his comb-back Windsor writing chair.

Wycombe Lath-back c 1840–1900 English
This was an armchair developed from the comb-back, with a heavy back rail and arms jointed into the back supports. The laths that took the place of spindles in earlier chairs were shaped to fit the back of the sitter, and although heavier they made a much more comfortable chair (see figure). A variation known as the 'Roman spindle' was given a rather more decorative appearance with spindles with simple turning.

The most popular of the lath-backs was the 'lath-and-baluster' which had a decorative splat in the back (see figure).

Writing chair type of Windsor chair with drawer (1780–90)
American Museum in Britain, Bath

Lath-back Windsor chair
(late 19th century)

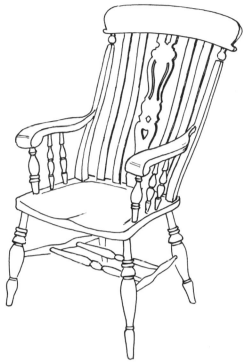

'Lath-and-baluster' Windsor chair
(late 19th century)

Wycombe Whites
Unstained chairs produced in the High Wycombe area and finished elsewhere.

Yorkshire chair This was a type of back-stool with arched, arcaded and carved rails which was first developed about 1620 in Yorkshire, Lancashire and Derbyshire, eventually spreading to many other regions. It was the ancestor of the later ladder-back chair. The usual type had two arched rails in the back, variations were restricted to the turning of the front legs and the details of carving. In a type believed to have developed in Derbyshire, the upper arcaded rail was connected to the lower one by two turned spindles. These chairs could be produced fairly quickly on the lathe, as chairs became more general articles of furniture, only the carving took extra time. After

the middle of the 17th century, the uprights of the back were sometimes ornamented with split balusters.

Soon the chairs were produced in many areas and continued to be made during the Commonwealth period, and in country districts well into the 18th century (see photograph overleaf).

A type made after the middle of the 17th century incorporated a carved mask in the middle of the top rail, which was said to be the head of Charles I. The name 'mortuary' given to them is a modern term. The chairs were no doubt intended as an expression of royalist sympathy.

X-chair These date from medieval times; 17th century examples still survive. See *Cofferer*.

Yorkshire chairs (17th and 18th centuries)
Victoria and Albert Museum

Chamfer The surface formed by removing an angle or edge by planing it away, usually on a leg (see figure).

Charles II (1660–85) The Restoration of Charles II to the throne acted as a parting of the ways between the traditional country craftsmen who continued to make the designs they had made throughout the early part of the 17th century, and went on making them during the 18th century as well, and the town craftsmen who developed new methods of construction learnt from continental craftsmen. Charles had spent a long time abroad and both he and his court had acquired new fashions in furnish-

ings, which they wished to continue and develop in England.

The late 17th century cabinet makers in towns produced new methods of veneering, enabling them to use imported woods not used by country workers. No longer was the construction of a particular piece of furniture obvious, nor was the wood from which it was made. Their furniture became smoother in appearance with a high polish, and not suitable for farmhouse or country cottage, where well tried designs in sturdy oak were still needed.

Cherry (*Prunus avium*) A hard fruitwood used from medieval times for much country

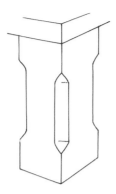

A chamfered leg

furniture. It is light reddish brown, and was particularly used in the 17th and 18th centuries for turned parts of chairs and tables and also for chests, table tops and chair seats. It polishes well and is resistant to warping.

CHEST

A wooden receptacle with a flat lid, made to stand on the floor. It is the only item of medieval furniture which has survived in any numbers.

Early types The earliest and most primitive form was the *dug-out chest*, the original 'trunk', dug out, with axe and adze, from a solid tree trunk, roughly cut to rectangular shape and fitted with a lid. Almost all the surviving examples are in cathedrals, churches and museums. The disadvantage of this type of construction was that as the trunk from which it was made dried out it was inclined to split.

This was also the case with the *Gothic* chests, dating from the 13th century, made of large

Riven oak carpenter-made chest (late 15th or early 16th century)
Ipswich Museum

planks fastened together with hand-forged nails or oak pins, a method which continued to be used in country areas until the 18th century. These chests were often decorated with chip carving with geometrical patterns or Gothic tracery. The pinning did not allow any movement in the wood, again resulting in splits across the grain.

A small chest from Ipswich Museum is shown (see photograph, page 93), which may be late 15th or early 16th century, but which is of a type made by carpenters since the 13th century. It is made of riven (not sawn) oak boards, with planked sides with tenon and pegged joints. The lid consists of three boards, the horizontal one passing through the side support, the other two angled, and it has a wooden pivot hinge. The wide stiles are extended downwards to form feet, one of the earliest ways of raising a chest off damp floors.

In early Tudor times the chest was still a most important item of furniture for use as a seat or a bed as well as for storage. A simple *boarded or plank chest* of six pieces of wood was in use, the sides being carried down lower than the front and back to form feet, often in the form of Gothic buttresses. Both this and the earlier types were often painted and gilded and

had iron straps both for further decoration and to strengthen them. The top was attached with wrought-iron strap hinges or iron wire staples linked together to form a hinge. Iron locks, sometimes as many as three, were fitted. Thinner boards were used in the 16th and 17th centuries, producing a lighter and smaller chest, often decorated with slight mouldings and low relief carving. These boarded chests continued to be made by carpenters for many years after the introduction of the panelled chests made by joiners (see figure).

Panelled chests These were developed in the 15th century and were in general use in the reign of Elizabeth I. The early type was carved with linenfold carving (see *Linenfold*), a style that was popular in the reign of Henry VIII and for many years afterwards. The example illustrated (see figure) has the extended uprights and Gothic shaped ends of earlier examples, but is of 16th century date. Many such chests with this 16th century carving have dates of the late 18th or early 19th century carved upon them, showing how the same styles were used for several centuries in country areas.

The panelled chest consists of two panelled

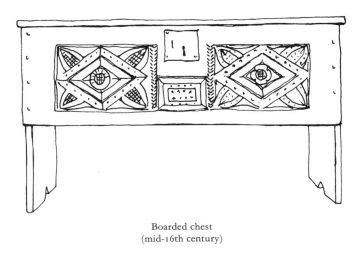

Boarded chest
(mid-16th century)

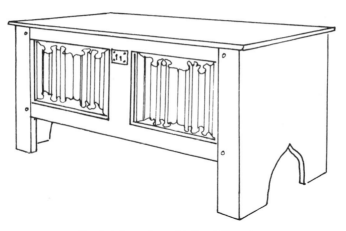

Panelled frame chest with linenfold carving
(early 16th century)

frames for a front and a back, jointed together with more framing and panels at the ends and flat plank lids with battens underneath which sometimes appear outside the lid when closed, or which were panelled to match the front.

Decoration Early frames are decorated with scratched mouldings (see *Mouldings*) which are not continuous, but which die out on the surface to leave a plain square edge. Another type of moulding used was the 'continuous run' variety; both were part of the solid framing, and continued to be used in country chests long after the fashion of mitring the mouldings came into general use about 1600. These mitred mouldings (each edge of the mouldings framing the panel was cut at an angle of 45°) were run on separate strips of oak, accurately fitted, glued and bradded in position, a method of decoration used up to the 18th century. Chests where the mitred mouldings form elaborate patterns are usually of late 17th century date.

Many chests were inlaid with grotesques and animals. Others, known as '*Nonsuch*' chests, were inlaid with coloured woods in the shape of a palace, said to be Henry VIII's Palace of Nonsuch in Surrey, later destroyed, but there is no authority for this. These were popular, but were very probably imported or made here by foreign craftsmen.

Carving on 16th century chests is often coarsely executed and profuse, a favourite early type having arcaded panels (see *Arcading*). These Elizabethan chests continued to be made in country districts throughout the 17th century, although construction and decoration became less solid, with improvements in joinery. Chests often had a small box or trough built in as part of the chest at one end near the top, for small objects or perhaps sweet-smelling herbs.

The chest illustrated from Ipswich Museum (see photograph) has a front carved with round arch arcading, the centre panel has the arcade infilled with a foliate design with tulips and rosettes and there is foliate carving on the rails. The top rail is incised with the date 1664, but in this country oak example the carver has reversed the figure 4.

American chests Chests of the same date with arcaded designs are found in America and there are many similarities in motifs used on American chests and those carved on 17th century English examples. Tulips are a

Carved oak chest with round arch arcading (1664)
Ipswich Museum

Painted dower chest (Pennsylvania Dutch, 1785)
American Museum in Britain, Bath

favourite flower, resulting from the Flemish craftsmen who worked in England and the Dutch settlers of the early colonies. They are seen in the Pennsylvania chest and the Connecticut chest shown here.

Most of the modern furniture research is devoted to trying to find the links between areas in England and the American colonies. The research is still in comparatively early stages, but an example of the type of information that is emerging is the double heart motif found on many chests and chair backs of 17th century date in Gloucestershire and the west country, which is also found on furniture attributed to the Guildford area of New Haven colony of Connecticut in America. The substantial lunette decoration (see *Lunette*) of

some American chests is a common motif in Somerset.

As in many countries, the Americans had the custom of providing a *dower* or hope chest for a prospective bride to hold the clothes, linen and blankets forming part of her dowry. American designs are often painted where carving or inlay would be used in England. The example illustrated (see photograph) from the American Museum at Bath is a Pennsylvania Dutch dower chest of 1785 date. The arcaded design is painted on a blue ground, with red painted hearts and tulips. The chest has three drawers below and brass handles.

An earlier Connecticut chest (see photograph) in oak of 1670–1690 date, also from the American Museum, has three panels, the side

Connecticut carved oak chest decorated with split spindles (1670–1690)
American Museum in Britain, Bath

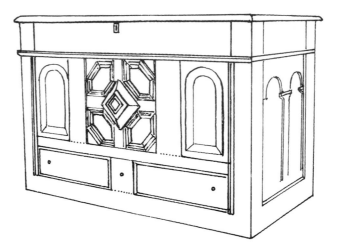

Chest with two drawers and arcaded panels (*c*.1660)

ones square and the centre panel octagonal, carved in low relief with stylized tulips. It has a hinged top and two drawers below. It is decorated with applied split spindles, painted black.

Tulip and sunflower designs were favourite carvings on the New England chests of this period. A type known as the Hadley chest from Massachusetts was highly carved all over with flowers and leaves in low relief, with incised lines curling around within the designs.

These American chests with drawers below are of a type known in England as a 'mule chest', the transitional stage between the chest and the chest-of-drawers, devised to solve the problem of searching at the bottom of a chest for articles. The English example (see figure) of a chest of about 1660 date has two drawers at the bottom, and arcaded panels on each side of the centre panel, and at each end. Blanket chests in England and Wales were generally made of elm or of cedarwood which was thought to be moth-proof.

Forerunner of the tin trunk Walter Rose explains in *The Village Carpenter* that no servant leaving a village for domestic service in the last century was properly equipped without her own box strongly made by the village carpenter. The making of this was a day's work by the carpenter, necessitating the planing of all the wood and the dovetailing of each angle. The finished box was fitted with lock and key, and iron handles at each end and was expected to last a lifetime. These were made until they came to be replaced by the tin trunk.
(See also *Ark; Carver and Carving; Coffer; hair-trunk* and *Standard*.)

CHEST OF DRAWERS

This was originally a 'chest with drawer'; the drawer or 'till' as it was first known was incorporated in the lower part of the chest. The main upper chest portion had panels carved in contemporary patterns, and it had one or two drawers beneath. This avoided the problem of finding objects at the bottom of a storage chest. Another name for this hybrid piece, which made its appearance at the end of the 16th century, is *mule chest*, but this is not a contemporary term. It was a rare piece of furniture until the middle of the 17th century, but continued to be made in country districts for the next hundred years or so (see figure).

At the same time the chest of drawers as we

Oak chest with two drawers; often described today as 'mule chest'
(mid-17th century)

know it today developed. The chest portion, made with the lid now fixed, also had a drawer, with the bank of lower drawers at first hidden behind cupboard doors. The whole was decorated with elaborate mitred mouldings (see *Mouldings*) in geometric patterns, which hid the real nature of the article, possibly for security reasons.

The oak example from Ipswich Museum (see photograph) is of mid-17th century date, and has one long drawer at the top, with the mouldings arranged to look like two drawers, a favourite treatment for drawer fronts, and three graduated drawers behind the panelled cupboard doors. It has applied split turned balusters on the stiles, a usual 17th century

Oak chest of drawers with panelled doors (mid-17th century)   *Ipswich Museum*

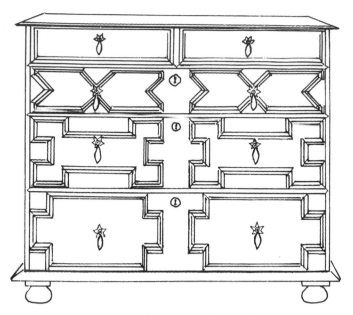

Chest of drawers, with drawers of
graduated size (*c*.1660)

Oak chest of drawers with cabriole feet
(18th century)

decoration. These were often stained black to look like ebony.

Early drawers had stout sides which were grooved to slide on runners fixed to the main carcase; rough dovetailing was attempted at the side joins. The bottom boards of the drawers were placed transversely and fixed with nails or dowels.

Drawers without doors By the second half of the 17th century the chest of drawers without doors was common in towns and this was one of the first pieces of furniture to be finished by the new technique of veneering. Many country homes however continued to use only chests and cupboards for storage well into the 18th century. No chests of drawers appear in probate inventories of a Devonshire village up to 1769. Chests *with* drawers are mentioned in Essex inventories of the second half of the 17th century.

The drawers are again graduated in size in the chest of about 1660 date (see figure) which has the original ball feet of the time and pear drop handles to the drawers. Often the feet of earlier pieces were extensions of the corner stiles. Bracket feet were often added later. Few early chests have the original feet, and few have the original handles to the drawers.

In the 18th century chests of drawers were still being made in oak with the panels in the 17th century style. The chest illustrated (see figure) has the cabriole foot which take it into the 18th century.

In the 18th century the sides of the drawers became thinner and side-runners were no longer used. The base of the drawer was built up on a piece of wood called a runner on which the drawer slid in and out. Dovetails became thinner and increased in number.

At first the chest of drawers was mounted on a solid base or on a stand with feet. The stands gradually became higher, enabling the bottom drawers to be reached more easily. The Charles

Oak chest of drawers on arcaded stand (Charles II)

II chest of drawers (see figure) has sunk panels without the elaborate mouldings of earlier examples, and is on an arcaded stand, which has a drawer in it.

The tallboy and the highboy During the 18th century the chest on a stand developed further into a *chest-upon-chest*, which was what it said it was, one chest of drawers on top of another slightly larger one. This was also known as a *tallboy*, which was also the name for a tall chest of drawers mounted on a stand which also had drawers. This was usually made with veneered fronts to the drawers, and was principally a cabinet maker's piece, made in towns. Plain country versions in oak were made, but would not have been too much in demand in country

homes with low ceilings. One oak example in Ipswich Museum is illustrated (see figure), the lower section having one long and two short drawers on square cut cabriole legs with shaped apron brackets. The top section has a flat top with an overhanging cornice. Later tallboys had pedimented tops.

Earlier William and Mary styles had six tall legs with inverted cup turnings, connected with curved stretchers, which during the 18th century became four cabriole legs, with pendant knobs indicating where two of the earlier legs would have been, rather like the small side tables of the period.

The tallboy had a longer life in America, where it was known as a *highboy* or in inventories as a 'high chest' or 'high chest of

Chest-upon-chest, or tallboy
(18th century) *Ipswich Museum*

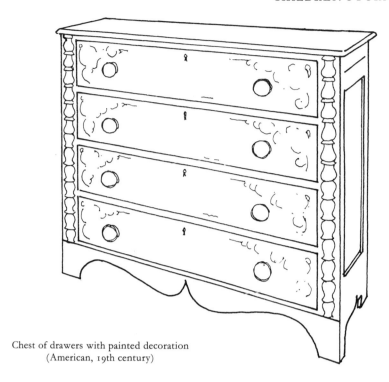

Chest of drawers with painted decoration
(American, 19th century)

drawers'. Plain versions in maple and pine were made in New England, the more ornamental varieties coming from Philadelphia. It continued in use in America long after it had gone out of fashion in England. It developed throughout the whole of the 18th century into a very popular and decorative piece of furniture. Graceful Chippendale styles in mahogany and walnut were richly carved and ornamented. It got higher and higher and needed specially made steps to reach the top drawers.

The bottom half of the highboy also appeared independently in America as the *lowboy*, used as a side table with drawers beneath, a dressing table or writing table. The highboy and lowboy were often made in matching versions.

Decoration Often late 18th century plain country-made chests of drawers in solid oak were decorated in simple fashion with a little inlay work in lighter woods, perhaps a band of walnut round the drawer fronts, or a star or rosette decorating each drawer.

In America a popular type (see figure) in cottage furniture was usually painted with floral designs and had split ball and reel turnings down the front stiles.

Chestnut (*Aesculus hippocastanum*) A soft, light wood, not satisfactory for the structure of furniture unless, as advised in Evelyn's *Sylva* (1662), it is first dipped in scalding oil and well pitched when he says it becomes extremely durable. It was used for carving and inlay work. It was also used for milkmaids' buckets before the introduction of galvanized pails.

Children's furniture Children's chairs have been produced in most of the styles made for adults at least since Tudor times. The earliest armchairs with panel backs were made in small versions for children, also the caquetoire chairs found in England and Scotland in the 16th and 17th centuries, carved with the same motifs as the adult versions.

High chairs were also made in the 17th century, in panel-back styles. Often great care was lavished on them; some are found with the back panel inlaid with holly and bog oak.

In the 18th and 19th centuries children's chairs continued to mirror adult styles, though as usual when these are found in country areas there is a time lag between them and those made earlier in towns. The chair with the mid-18th century style back (see figure) from Lancaster Museum, is of early 19th century date.

The chair of the smoker's bow Windsor type (see photograph) from Reading Museum has been used by at least three generations. It has a wooden lid for placing over a pot in the seat. The legs are probably beech, the seat elm and the arms ash. A bar would have been inserted in the holes through the arms to prevent the child falling out.

Elegant children's Windsors in bow back and scroll back designs (see *Chair* section) are found in the 19th century. A child's version of the Mendlesham chair is in Ipswich Museum, just as graceful as the larger version. The Windsor chairmakers of Rockley in Nottinghamshire produced small yew, ash and beech chairs in the middle of the 19th century in the pattern of the Lancashire Windsors.

The wing chair (see photograph overleaf) with the pot-hole in the seat and tray in front was made in Wales. It is in elm and was probably made by Isaac Lewis, carpenter of Bryngwyn, near Raglan, Monmouthshire who died in 1830.

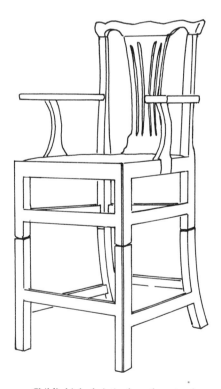

Child's high chair (early 19th century)

Child's chair of the smoker's bow Windsor type (19th century)
Museum of English Rural Life, Reading

Many American children's chairs remain from an early date, very well made; perhaps because American children always lived with the family and were not banished to the nursery as in so many British homes. A higher standard of design and workmanship was therefore demanded. American children's chairs of Windsor design are very elegant. An arch-back chair is illustrated (see figure), with wide splayed legs which gave a greater stability.

About 1800 a corrective chair for children appeared, designed to make them sit up straight at the table. It was designed by Sir Astley Paston Cooper, an eminent surgeon, also surgeon to the King, and was a very high chair with a straight back. Its popularity was sufficient for it to appear in the Wycombe chair catalogues of the 1860s as the Astley-Cooper chair.

While many country chairs in Scotland were low chairs, built to protect the occupants from the smoke of peat fires, there are many

Child's wing chair (Welsh, early 19th century)
National Museum of Wales

Child's arch-back
Windsor high-chair
(American, 19th century)

Child's low chair
(Scotland, 19th century)

especially low for children, some copies of adults' chairs, and others especially craftsmen-made for children. A child's chair from Perthshire is illustrated (see figure).
(See also *Baby walker, Cradle* and *Stool.*)

Chip carving A type of carving used from the 13th to the 17th century. Geometrical patterns were chipped out by the carpenter.

CLOCKS

Only the wealthier farmers would have had a clock of any sort until the middle of the 18th century or more likely the early 19th century. In the small country homes of Britain, certainly from about 1840 onwards, the household clock would most likely have been mass-produced in America. For this reason it seems

sensible to deal first with these imported clocks before discussing the long case or 'grand-father' clocks produced in Britain, although these date back to the 17th century.

American clocks Clockmaking had begun in the New England states of America by 1750. Most of the early clockmakers also made furniture and tools and were blacksmiths as well. Many of the early clocks had all wood movements. In the 19th century the new industrial techniques led to the production of enormous numbers of cheap but reliable clocks, principally in Connecticut and Mass-achusetts.

These American clocks were found in almost every farmhouse and cottage in Britain from the middle of the 19th century, largely taking the place of the grandfather clock in its

Mass-produced clock
(American, 19th century)
Museum of English Rural Life, Reading

oak case. It was one of the earliest examples of the success of American mass production, and exporting and selling tactics. There were 8-day or 30-hour clocks with brass movements, weight-driven, in rectangular cases, which stood on a bracket on the wall, or which could be hung on the wall as a wall clock. There was also a spring-driven clock in a case of Gothic design. Many of the designs were not painted but applied by transfer to save money.

The American clock illustrated (see photograph) belonged to a Cambridgeshire couple, who acquired it in 1876 when they were married, and it was in constant use until recently. It is now in the Reading Museum of Rural Life. It has a polished wood case and a decoration of fruit and leaves on the glass. There are many of these 19th century American clocks still giving good service in the country homes of Britain today.

Dutch clocks These were popular in country homes in the middle of the 19th century, when grandfather clocks could not be afforded. They had white-painted dials ornamented with bunches of flowers, and an unprotected pendulum and weights, showing what an English clock looked like before it was put in a long wooden case.

Long case clocks These are also known as long sleeve clocks, tall case clocks or grandfather clocks, the latter name having been given to them towards the end of the 19th century. This type of clock in a plain oak case first appeared after 1680, but as we have seen, clocks of any sort were not items of furniture which would have been found in small country homes until at earliest the middle of the 18th century.

At first the long case clock had only one hour hand, but by 1700 the minute hand had been added and grandfather clocks with two hands were general. Country clockmakers continued to make both grandfather and the earlier types of brass *lantern, bird-cage* or *Cromwellian* clocks with the hour hand only, long after London firms ceased to make this type. These earlier brass lantern clocks stood on a wall bracket with pendulum and weight exposed, and were also called *bracket* clocks.

Country long case clocks were rarely over 2 m (about 7 ft) in height and many were smaller to accommodate low farmhouse ceilings.

The 30-hour clock had both the going and striking mechanism driven by one weight attached to an endless chain, by which it was wound up, being pulled up by hand without any key.

The 8-day grandfather clock had the going and the striking movements on separate trains, driven by separate weights which are attached to gut lines, and were wound up by a key.

The earliest clocks had square brass or white metal dials, which were often engraved with quaint and interesting designs. The name of the clockmaker and the town or village in which he worked are almost certain to be engraved on the dial. By the early 19th century a cheaper variety of clock was made with a white enamelled dial, often painted with flowers or landscape patterns.

The cases of country clocks were mostly in oak, without much ornament, occasionally a banding of other wood. They usually had a square head, sometimes an ornamental scrolled head, or, after 1735 an arched head. The shape of the top of the door in the trunk usually followed the shape of the head, the door in the trunk of early clocks being square at the top, and later doors having a shaped top. The clock illustrated is an 8-day clock with a square top to the door, a scrolled head with small turned columns and a banding of contrasting wood on the door as the only other ornament. It was made by Thomas Pearce of Chard in Somerset (see figure). Country clocks from the north of England tended to have broader cases than those in the south and were more ornamented.

In the earliest models the head is often removable in its entirety by lifting it upwards in grooves and there is no hinged door. More suitable where ceilings were low was the later model where the head slid off forwards, and also had a hinged door in the front of the dial, opening outwards, which allowed the hands of the clock to be adjusted for winding.

Often the case seems older than the works, but this is because country clockmakers clung to the old plain designs and were at least twenty years behind London fashions. New works were often put into old cases. In the second half of the 18th century, when mahogany became

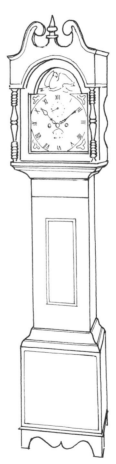

8-day long case clock. The country example has a scrolled head and square top door (West Country; late 18th or early 19th century)

popular, ox-blood or other stain was some-times used to colour oak cases to look like mahogany. In American long case or 'tall' clocks, the plain pine cases were usually painted, sometimes with deep red buttermilk paint. In many early tall clocks much of the mechanism was imported from England.

While there were many clockmakers in country towns and villages all over England in the late 18th and early 19th centuries, some of them very well known names, their numbers gradually diminished. The long case clock continued to be popular for many years in country districts, although it went out of fashion in London in the late 18th century. Even if there was a local clockmaker, towards the end of the 19th century it had become practicable to obtain the mechanisms from central warehouses in towns, and to put it in a case made by a local cabinet maker. Clock-makers had usually employed others to make the cases for them.

Tavern clocks In 1797 William Pitt imposed a tax on all clocks and watches, which had the result of large easily read clocks being installed in inns and other public buildings to provide the time for travellers and others who could no longer own a watch or clock. These came to be known as 'Act of Parliament' or 'tavern' clocks. The Act was repealed in 1798 as it was so unpopular, but this type of clock is still given these names.

Cock bead
See *Mouldings*

Coffer A small portable medieval chest, with a rounded lid, designed to house money and valuables. It was usually covered with leather or other material. The term is freely used for other forms of chest, such as the ark for the storage of flour, or the 'coffer bach' or Bible box of Wales (see *Ark; Box*). A trussing coffer was fitted with rings for lifting and easier transportation.

Cofferer The craftsman who made coffers. He was originally a leather worker, as most of the coffers were in wood covered with leather. As an expert in covering wood with other materials, he later made leather-covered chairs, and chairs and stools covered with various fabrics, often rich and colourful. In particular he made the X-shaped chair of Tudor times, known as the coffer-maker's chair. This was of Flemish origin, and had a strong framework, usually of beech. The seat had webbing or canvas across the X-frame, on the lines of a modern camp stool, on which a loose cushion could be placed. Some of the lighter chairs could be folded.

Column A turned part of a piece of furniture in the shape of a classical column, with straight sides, usually on a leg or stretcher.

Continuous run moulding
See *Chest; Moulding*

Cornice The projecting top of a piece of furniture, *eg*, the top of an 18th century bureau or cupboard.

Cotswold school This was the name of a group of designers and craftsmen – notably Ernest Gimson and Sidney and Ernest Barnsley – who set up a workshop near Cirecester in the Cotswolds in 1893, inspired by the ideas of William Morris (see *Morris*). They produced well-designed, well-made furniture, aimed at keeping alive the best traditions of country craftsmanship which Morris felt had been lost during the latter years of the Victorian age of mass production. They were instrumental in handing down William Morris's ideas to the 20th century. An example of a Gimson version of a ladder-back chair is shown on page 63.

Cradle The earliest beds for babies were probably of basket work, and cradles of this type have been in use until comparatively recent times (see *Basketry*).

Pine cradle with beech stand (late 19th century)
Museum of English Rural Life, Reading

Of the wooden varieties there are two main types to be found. One which dates from medieval times has the cradle slung between two trestle type posts, joined by a stretcher rail. The example illustrated (see photograph) is of late 19th century date, made of pine, with a slatted bottom; the stand is of beech. The unsatisfactory nature of this variety is apparent, as it has been necessary to put rockers under the main body of the cradle at some time, so that it could be rocked on the floor. It was found that energetic babies fell out when rocking the cradle too fast on the stand.

17th century cradles of panelled oak or elm, with or without a shaped hood, had either plain rockers or rockers with slight ornamental curves. The panels are usually plain, the only ornament being the turned knobs at the foot

111

CRADLE

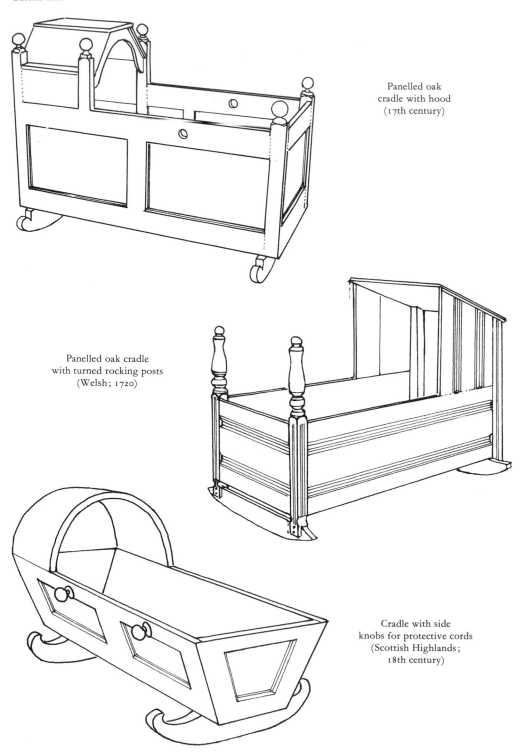

Panelled oak
cradle with hood
(17th century)

Panelled oak cradle
with turned rocking posts
(Welsh; 1720)

Cradle with side
knobs for protective cords
(Scottish Highlands;
18th century)

and sometimes at the head (see figure). These cradles are often found carved with initials and a date.

An oak example from Wales is also shown (see figure), with turned rocking posts and moulded panels; it is of 1720 date.

Holes at the side of a cradle were intended for a cord across to protect the baby. Sometimes there were knobs at the sides, so plaited wool could be wound round them and fastened across the cradle (see figure). The example illustrated comes from the Scottish Highlands.

Hoods were sometimes made of a piece of bent wood. Some of the hoods were hinged either at the side or at the head to give greater freedom when moving the baby. A Cromwellian example from Devon at the time of the Civil War had a useful secret compartment in the hood. Occasionally there was a small cupboard incorporated in the cradle to house a pewter pot.

Cresting The carved decoration on the top rail of a chair (see figure), sometimes perforated.

Cromwellian A term applied to furniture of about the time of the Commonwealth period of Puritan rule in England of 1649–1660, under Oliver Cromwell. The furniture typical of this period was austere and carving was at a minimum. The main forms of decoration approved of by the Puritans were turning and the decoration of the leather chairs of the

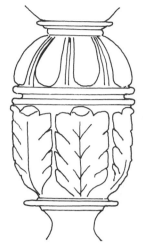

Cup and cover carving

period with brass studs, the latter being functional.
(See *Cromwellian chair* in the *Chair* section.)

Cross-banding
See *Banding*

Cup and cover A carved decoration applied to legs, bedposts and court cupboard supports in the Elizabethan period. The top of the bulb is carved to resemble the cover and the lower part the cup (see figure).

CUPBOARD

Originally, simply a cup-board, a shelf or stand for plates and cups, a common article of furniture in Tudor or Elizabethan inventories. Many farmers had 'learned also to garnish their cupboards with plate' according to William Harrison in his *Description of England, 1577–87* and the term cupboard was used for an open structure of this type throughout the 16th century.

Any enclosed part of these early cupboards which had a door was known as an *aumbry* or almery. Inventories listed cupboards 'with aumbries'. This term came to mean a food

Cresting, the carved decoration on the top rail of a chair (17th century)

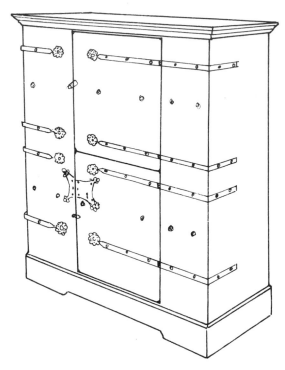

Food cupboard or hutch of planked construction
(early 16th century)

stand. The latter were the ancestors of many cupboards where the almoner of a great house kept food for distribution to the poor.

Small hanging cupboards found in churches, which also contained bread for the poor, were called *dole* cupboards. Open dole shelves often served the same purpose.

A term applied to late medieval cabinets or cupboards with shelves on which food was placed ready to be tasted before being served was *credence* cupboards.

Food cupboards These were also known as *hutches* and had various methods of ventilation. The earliest were made by carpenters and were of the same plank construction as the early chests, and had doors pierced with Gothic tracery to ventilate the inside (see figure). Later types were framed. An early example from Ipswich has two doors with diamond lat-

ticed panels for ventilation (see photograph).

On the west coast of Scotland where wood was scarce, food cupboards were often ventilated with wickerwork sides on wooden frames.

Sometimes the front was largely composed of turned balusters or spindles. In the latter half of the 16th century food cupboards were also known as *livery* cupboards, liveries originally being the rations of food and drink provided for the staff of a large household at night, so these cupboards are often found listed among bedroom furniture in inventories. The hanging livery cupboard illustrated (see photograph) is of 17th century date and comes from Kent. It is made of oak, inlaid with holly and bog oak across the front and round the edge. It has two rows of 15 turned bars; seven in the middle of each row form doors on pivots.

Livery cupboards could be open or partially enclosed by doors. Like the earlier hutches

An early food
cupboard with diamond
latticed panels
Ipswich Museum

Hanging livery
cupboard (17th century)
Victoria and Albert

they could take the form of standing cup-boards, hanging cupboards or cupboards on stands. The latter were the ancestors of many grander cabinets on stands which became so popular in the 18th and 19th centuries, as by the 17th century, when livery rations were no longer customary, this type of cupboard was used for many other purposes.

Many cupboards were simply doors fitted to recesses built into the farmhouse walls, usually near the fireplace to keep the contents dry. An oak food cupboard front from Suffolk is illustrated (see photograph), with a central opening door, decorated with punched pier-ced work and dated 1639. A cupboard from Old Sturbridge Village, Massachusetts, also

has punched work decorating the upper doors (see photograph opposite).

Fine late 18th century examples of bread and food cupboards in elm and yew are found in North Wales, survivors of an article of furniture in use in the Middle Ages. They are standing types having panelled doors, with rows of small turned spindles for ventilation in the top half, and either all drawers or a com-bination of drawers and cupboards below.

A still later 19th century example from New Mexico, a 'trasteros', used for storing clothing, food and household utensils, has two rows of spindles for ventilation in each door, and can be seen in the New Mexico living room at the American Museum at Bath (see photograph).

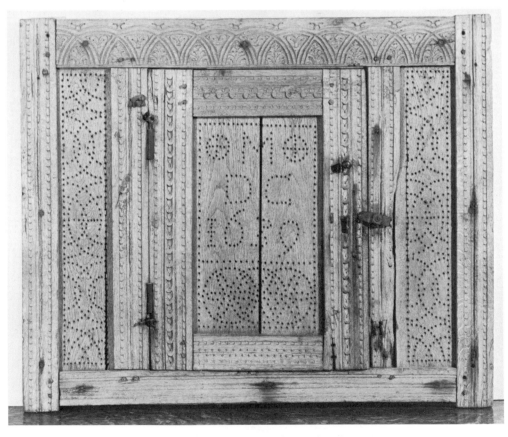

Oak food cupboard with punched pierced work (1639)
Ipswich Museum

American cupboard with punched pierced work
Old Sturbridge Village, Massachusetts

New Mexican trasteros used for
household storage (19th century)
American Museum in Britain, Bath

Court cupboards By the middle of the 16th century a structure of several shelves (usually three) for the display of plate was called a *court cupboard* (while the term *buffet* was more probably used if it was associated with food), the humble cottage still probably being satisfied with a single 'pottshelfe'. The top shelf of most forms of cupboard was covered with a piece of tapestry or carpet, green being a favourite colour. The drinking pots were kept on the lowest shelf – 'the pot borde'. This court cupboard became one of the most popular and highly decorated pieces of display furniture in the Elizabethan home. The shelves were supported at the back corners by flat posts and at the front by carved bulbous columns, which gave place to more slender baluster turned supports in the 17th century. Under the middle shelf there was usually a drawer in the frieze (see figure overleaf).

The upper section of a court cupboard might be fitted with a canted cupboard, and the bottom section could be enclosed with doors. Very similar 17th century examples are found in America, with an enclosed storage section either in the top or bottom half. They are of a

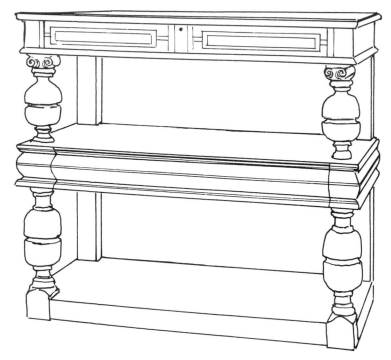

Court cupboard (*c.*1660)

sturdier appearance than the English examples and decorated with applied and often ebonized mouldings and spindles.

Some court cupboards were gilded or painted, but more usually they were finished with a clear varnish; they remained popular until the end of the 17th century.

Press A completely enclosed cupboard, fitted with a door or doors, in the 17th century was called a *press*, sometimes a 'close press'. Earlier very large presses were also called '*armoires*'. One form of press for use in the hall or dining room had large doors on the lower half, while the upper part was slightly recessed to form a narrow shelf and divided into three compartments, with doors on at least two. The top projected to form a roof and was supported by two turned bulbous columns. By the reign of Charles I these columns tended to disappear, and only turned knobs were a reminder of their

former use. The hall cupboard illustrated from Suffolk, of mid-17th century date, has a central door in the lower half with incised lozenge ornament, while the upper storey has two doors, again with a central lozenge ornament to each, and two baluster supporting pillars (see photograph).

Similar presses are found in America of the same date, the top part often with splayed sides, and cupboards or drawers in the bottom half. The split balusters used in decoration are usually painted black.

The other form of press was taller and had a flush front, usually broken up by panelling, with one central door or two doors hung at the sides. This was for the storage of linen, eventually becoming what we now call a wardrobe. Late 17th century cupboards of great size are often dated. The press shown (see photograph overleaf) in the Victoria and Albert Museum, came from a farm cottage in

Hall cupboard with incised lozenge ornament (mid-17th century)
Ipswich Museum

Oak press (17th century)
Victoria and Albert Museum

Carved two-piece cupboard,
'*cwpwrdd deuddarn*' (Welsh; 1702)
National Museum of Wales

The three-piece cupboard, *'cwpwrdd tridarn'* (Welsh; 1690)

Northamptonshire. It is a good oak example of the high quality of country craftsmanship in the second quarter of the 17th century. Made by a joiner, the front is of framed and panelled construction, the stiles which form the legs decorated with fluting, the horizontal members decorated with flat strapwork in relief against a hatched background. It would have been described in contemporary inventories as a 'wainscott presse to hang thereon clothes'. Inside, in the upper part, are eleven wooden pegs for hanging clothes, which could also be placed flat in the chest-like lower section.

The press was introduced into Wales in the 16th century and became known as *cwpwrdd*
deuddarn – the two-piece cupboard. It developed carvings of the uprights and the lower rail characteristic of Welsh furniture. The example illustrated (see photograph) comes from Monmouthshire, is carved with palmated chain patterns and is dated 1702. By the middle of the 17th century an extra canopy and shelf for the display of pewter and earthenware was added producing the *cwpwrdd tridarn* – the three-piece cupboard, unique to Wales (see figure). As in England by 1700 the balusters which supported the canopy were replaced by pendants. The popularity of the *deuddarn* in Welsh farmhouses lasted well into the 19th century.

The press in America The very large 17th century *Dutch kas*, a similar solid type of cupboard to the flush-fronted English press, made by early settlers in America, usually had shelves inside, and when not decorated with panels and applied mouldings, was painted with designs of fruit, birds and flowers in a variety of colours. Like the early chests and tables, the kas could be dismantled to facilitate moving this large piece of furniture. They continued to be made well into the 19th century as was a similar massive piece of furniture introduced by German and Swiss settlers in Pennsylvania in the 17th century and called a *schrank*. This was sometimes made in walnut or cherry, or was painted with colourful designs of fruit and flowers. Like the Elizabethan court cupboard it was a status symbol as well as a storage unit.

Spice-cupboard (18th century)

Small cupboards At the other end of the scale, small cupboards to hang on farmhouse walls in many shapes are found on both sides of the Atlantic. Those fitted with small drawers inside are *spice-cupboards* or boxes, and stored

Pennsylvanian wall cupboard (18th century)
American Museum in Britain, Bath

the valuable herbs and spices used in country kitchens. Some are decorated with mitred mouldings (see figure opposite); in the 18th century examples they may have an arched top.

The Pennsylvanian wall cupboard illus-(see photograph) is of 18th century date and is in the American Museum at Bath. It has two doors with raised panels, and a scalloped apron. It was originally painted dark red.

Corner cupboards These are triangular and probably originated as simple fitted shelves across the corner of a room. They are first mentioned at the beginning of the 18th century, and could be either free-standing or hanging, flat-fronted and panelled or bow-fronted from the end of the 18th century.

When the standing variety was in two parts, the upper part was sometimes glazed to display the china and glass on its shelves. The early 19th century cupboard illustrated (see photograph) from South Wales is in oak.

The space-saving hanging cupboards were especially popular in country districts throughout the 18th and 19th centuries (see figures). All types had shelves, often grooved at the

Oak corner cupboard
(Welsh; early 19th century)
National Museum of Wales

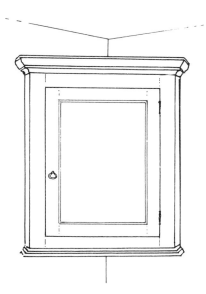

Hanging corner cupboard (18th century)

back to support standing plates. The back-boards were usually painted green on the inside. At the end of the 18th century the fronts were often bowed and inlaid with borders. Examples are found in Wales and the border

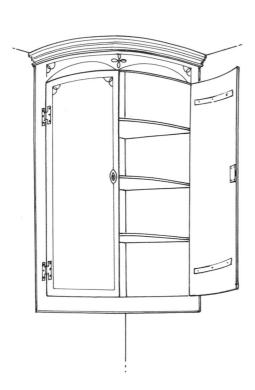

Bow-fronted hanging corner cupboard
(late 18th century)

Hanging corner cupboard with pediment
(late 18th century)

counties in oak with bandings of mahogany and inlaid floral decoration (see figure).

Many hanging cupboards had small drawers beneath or inside them. Flat-fronted cupboards were sometimes pedimented (see figure).

Cyma curve The edge of a piece of furniture, such as the side of a dresser, or a moulding or cornice, having a wavy or curved profile (see figure).

Cypress
See *Cedar*

Deal This is a general term for pine, especially Scots Pine (*Pinus sylvestris*) and the wood of various coniferous trees; it is a softwood, principally used for carcase work, drawer linings and the backs of case furniture. The wood is honey to red-brown in colour.

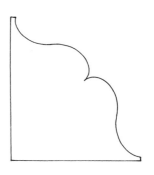

Cyma curve

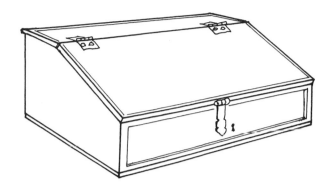

Desk box
(18th century)

Desk (or Desk box) In the medieval period this was a box with a sloping top or lid, hinged at the top, used for writing or reading. It was very like the later type of 17th century Bible box (see *Box*). Such desks were portable and were placed on tables in the 16th and early 17th centuries (see figure). By the second half of the 17th century they were being made with stands, with the sloping top used for writing when opened down flat, the hinge being at the bottom.
(See also *Bureau*.)

Dogwood (*Cornus sanguinea*) A very hard, light yellow sapwood with yellowish-red heart, used for inlays in the 16th and 17th centuries.

Double heart motif A decorative carving found on chests and chair backs of 16th and 17th century date, consisting of two hearts, their tops adjoining (see figure). It is a common form of decoration on furniture from Gloucestershire and the West country, but it is also found on early Pilgrim furniture attributed to the Guildford area of the New Haven colony of Connecticut in America.

Dough bin
See *Bread trough*

Dovetail A method used by a joiner to join the sides of drawers by interlocking projections, used from the middle of the 17th century onwards (see figure). The earliest dovetails were few in number and rather crude, the projections being cut right through the wood, so that the end grain of the wood showed on both sides of the angle. This was known as 'through dovetailing' (see figure). In

Double heart motif used in carving chests
and chair backs (16th and 17th centuries)

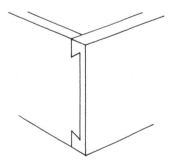

Early dovetailing (mid-17th century)

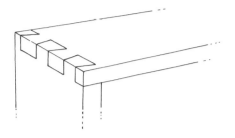

'Through dovetailing' (mid-17th century)

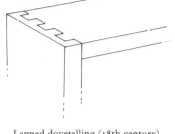

Lapped dovetalling (18th century)

the 18th century dovetails became more numerous and smaller, and the 'stopped dovetail' or 'lapped dovetail' was used (see figure). The slots for the projections were not cut right through so that the front of the drawer was left plain for decoration by applied mouldings and veneering. The lapped dovetail became standard construction for cabinet makers to use for case furniture in the 18th century. Most dovetails were cut by hand until the present century.

Dowel A wooden headless pin or peg used to join furniture. It was inserted through a mortise and tenon joint (see *Joint*) to hold it fast. Sometimes called a 'trennell' or 'tree-nail'. Squared and tapered dowels were hammered into round holes for greater strength and were often made of green wood. They are found to be warped when removed from old furniture. The pegs were trimmed off level with the frame after insertion.

Grooved drawer construction
(late 16th/early 17th century)

Drawer Drawers were known in the 16th century, when they were called tills or drawing boxes. Simple forms, nailed together, are found resting on the framework in cupboards and tables.

In the late 16th or early 17th century, grooves were cut in the side of the drawer and a corresponding projection fitted to the framework on which the drawer could run (see figure). This type of drawer has been revived in this century. Drawers became more plentiful from the 17th century onwards, the sides and front being joined by dovetail joints. By the 18th century the drawer moved on strips of wood attached to the base of the drawer itself, and cabinet makers introduced a dust board which was fixed between the drawers.

DRESSER

The word comes from the Norman French *dressoir* and the dresser was originally a sideboard or side table on which one 'dressed' the food before serving it. In the 17th century the dresser acquired shelves above it for the display of pewter and delftware, which was a logical development, enabling dishes to be near at hand while food was served. In some parts of the country a dresser is still known as a delft-rack.

The earliest dressers were side tables with drawers beneath, as in the example illustrated (see figure) of the second half of the 17th century. It has the same type of decoration as on chests of drawers of the same date,

Oak dresser with geometrical designs and applied split turnings (*c*.1680)

geometrical designs and applied split turnings. The front legs are turned and the back ones left straight.

This type of dresser without shelves above was in use during the next two centuries, eventually becoming a dresser of all drawers of varying sizes as in the example illustrated (see photograph), an elongated chest of drawers.

In many parts of the country the bottom part of a dresser with shelves is always a separate piece, especially in the north, the shelves either standing free on the top of the lower part or else hanging on, or built into, the walls.

Many dressers of the type illustrated have had later tops added to provide shelves which are of a later date than the bottom. Many

Dresser without shelves, having drawers or varying sizes   *Farmers' Weekly*

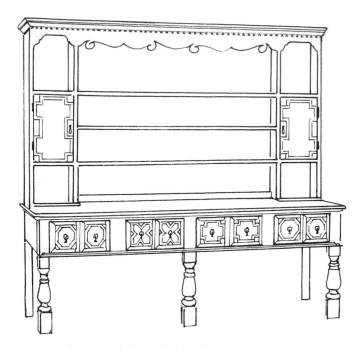

Dresser with decorated drawer front and top (*c.*1670)

Oak dresser with arcaded doors and decorated apron
(William and Mary, *c.*1689)

Dresser with carved frieze, and a pot board   *Farmers' Weekly*

examples with shelves originally open at the back have had back boards fitted; back boards when present have often been renewed. They are sometimes covered with red lead and painted black to ward off damp and pests.

The number of legs on early dressers varied according to the length of the dresser, sometimes there were four, sometimes six or even eight.

The dresser with cupboards When shelves were added it soon became convenient to incorporate cupboards as well, as in the 17th century example illustrated (see figure), which

has a decorated drawer front and top. It is rare to find two dressers exactly the same, there are so many variations in the decorated tops, the arrangement of drawers and cupboards and the turning of the legs. Even the particular wood used gives a different appearance to each dresser. Pine, elm and fruitwoods were used as well as oak.

Guard rails along shelves are common to prevent the dishes slipping off. Rails with bobbin and spindle turnings as well are found in the midlands and north.

In the later William and Mary example (see figure) the two doors have an arcaded design,

Dresser with shaped fielded panels (Lancashire, mid-18th century)

and the eight legs are joined by stretchers. It has a decorated top and the apron under the drawers is also decorated. A door at each side is usual in dressers of this date and a pot board on top of the stretchers was often present, on which larger vessels and dishes could be placed (see photograph).

In the 18th century one of the developments in the design of dressers was the increase in drawer space, shown in the mid-18th century Lancashire dresser (see figure), which has a central door in the shelf portion, and also a central door in the bottom, both with shaped fielded panels. Dressers became massive as the century advanced, growing into the plain and capacious varieties found in 19th century farmhouses.

Cabriole legs are found on 18th century dressers, particularly in Lancashire, and there are dressers with built-in clocks, which are also thought to originate in the north. These sometimes have small spice drawers on each side as in the example shown (see photograph).

Regional characteristics Many dressers are referred to as Welsh dressers which are in fact English. While the dresser has always been a very popular item in Welsh farmhouses, the Welsh varieties do not differ in a great respect from the English ones. Greater decoration is usual with pierced aprons and scrolled sides, as in the early 18th century example shown (see figure overleaf). An example from Swansea is illustrated under *Welsh furniture*. Dressers with cupboards at the bottom are thought to be found mostly in the north of Wales, the south and west having the lower portion left open and fitted with an apron piece.

The Welsh dressers for the most part are compact affairs, as were dressers in the west of

North country dresser with built-in clock and spice drawers (18th century)
Farmers' Weekly

Oak dresser with scrolled sides (Welsh; *c.*1725)

England. In Devon the top portion was often enclosed by doors as well, so that the shelves were only visible when the doors were open.

In his description of old Cornish farm-houses A. K. Hamilton Jenkins tells how the kitchen dresser was the showpiece of the home and would be carefully arranged according to fashion, with glasses at the top, the tea set next with larger plates at the back. Bowls and larger basins stood at the side, with a strip of linen under them.

Egg-and-reel A type of turning used in the 17th century, especially on the legs of gate-leg tables (see figure).

Elizabethan A term applied to furniture of

Egg-and-reel turning (17th century)

the style of the reign of Queen Elizabeth I (1558–1603), characterized by the richness of its carving, especially in the large bulbous turnings of the legs of chairs, tables and court cupboard supports.

Elm (*Ulmus procera*) This light reddish-brown wood is used in much country furniture for chair seats, table tops and for the coffins made in the past by most country carpenters, for even Chippendale was a funeral furnisher as well as a cabinet maker. It is a hard-wearing wood, attaining a good polish, but it warps easily and is subject to woodworm. The older the elm, the deeper the colour of the wood produced. The great size to which the elm grows made it particularly useful for large tables. It was also popular with wheelwrights and used for waggon building and other work.

In view of the number of elms cut down in the 1970s due to Dutch Elm disease, the words of Walter Rose in his book *The Village Carpenter* are significant, when he tells how in his day after an elm was felled it was held that the log should lie at least a year before being sawn – otherwise the plank would warp badly – but that it should not lie too long, as after about two years a whiteness would strike the interior to the detriment of the timber.

Feet
See *Ball foot (bun foot and onion foot); Bracket foot; Cabriole leg; Hoof foot; Spanish foot*

Fielded A panel with the flat centre portion bevelled at the edges, so that the panel appears to be raised, popular in the 17th century particularly for cupboard fronts.

Finial A terminal knob on furniture. Two popular finials in America, principally seen on the front and back uprights of chairs are the lemon finial and the mushroom finial (see figures).

Fitted furniture In small country homes

fitted furniture has always made the most of shortages of space. Some of the earliest medieval beds were boxed-in alcoves, often beneath stairways, and these continued to be made until the 19th century.

Cupboards were frequently doors fronting alcoves built into the brickwork, especially near fireplaces where it was needed to keep goods dry.

Many benches were built in as seats in window alcoves and in ingle-nook fireplaces.

Floor covering
See *Carpets*

Lemon finial (American; 17th century)

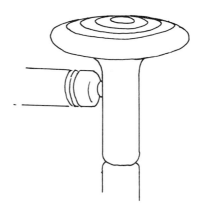

Mushroom finial (American; 17th century)

Fluting, a type of gouged channel carving
(17th and 18th centuries)

Fluting Gouged channels carved on legs and stiles of 17th and 18th century furniture (see figure).

Footwarmer This was a small three-sided box, like a small wooden stool, which held a metal container for hot cinders or burning charcoal. It usually had decorative vents at the sides and top, and sometimes a guard-rail at the open side. The type shown here (see figure) was probably used as a foot-stool, while another type was four-sided, with a carrying handle.

Form A long backless seat; see *Bench*.

FRAMER

The craftsman who was responsible for assembling the various parts of a Windsor chair on a low bench, known as a framing block. After they were smoothed, the parts were joined by socketing the legs, bows and arms into holes drilled in the seat, the whole glued and wedged together. The finished article was then stained. This is now a mechanical process, but formerly it was a lengthy business demanding high skill. The chairs were cleaned with nitric acid, then heated in a solution of wood chips to stain them, grain being added by a variety of combs. Some of the cheaper chairs were polished with linseed oil, some waxed, some painted, or coated with shellac polish or highly polished and then dulled with pumice powder. Some were left untouched 'in the white'.

The framer had a more extensive tool kit than any of the other workers. It included a metal framing hammer, spokeshaves, scrapers and wooden braces and bits used to bore the holes to take various parts. An average Windsor chair has about thirty mortises to be bored. The ends of the parts were dried in an oven to prevent further shrinking. When they were glued and hammered into the holes of the green wood this would gradually tighten as it seasoned, and the joints became more secure.

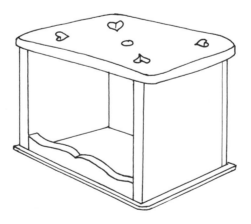

Footwarmer with decorative vents (19th century)

Wedges were also inserted to tighten the joints even further, making a chair that seldom develops loose joints even after many years of very hard wear.
(See also *Tools*.)

Frieze The band below the cornice on a piece of furniture, or the upper horizontal member or rail.

Gadrooning A repetitive edge of fluting, convex in form, sometimes in S-form, used on the borders of stools and the edges of tables in the 16th and 17th centuries (see figure).

Gothic A term first used in the 17th century to describe the style of decoration and building used principally in churches and cathedrals of the 12th to 15th centuries. It was originally used as a term of abuse, as this style of decoration was wrongly thought to have been originated by the Goths, the vanquishers of the Roman Empire. It is characterized by pointed arches and tracery, all designs found on the furniture of this time (see figure).

Gougework A decoration formed by scooping out a pattern with a semi-circular gouge, found on the rails of chairs and chests of 17th century date (see figure).

Grotesque A form of carving used in the late 16th and early 17th centuries to ornament chair backs and chests with fantastic monsters and figures.

Guilloche A border carving of interlaced circles of ribbon effect, used from the 16th–18th centuries (see figure).

Hadley chest
See *Chest*

Hair-trunk An 18th and 19th century travelling trunk, in various sizes, covered with skins, with the pelt outside, associated with the coaching age.

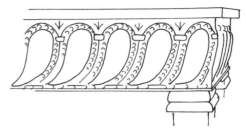

Gadrooning, a carved decoration
(16th and 17th centuries)

Gothic pierced panel

Gougework, a carved decoration found on rails of chairs and chests (17th century)

Guilloche carving (16th to 18th centuries)

135

Inverted heart and pear drop handles
(17th century)

William and Mary, and Queen Anne handles

Chippendale handle with pierced back plate
(18th century)

Handle The handles on 17th century drawers are often not the original handles. These may have been fixed by two wires through the drawer front, bent over on the inside of the drawer to hold the handle in place. Later wrought iron nails were used.

Early types of handles were simple iron rings, perhaps shaped to an inverted heart, or else a simple pear drop or tear drop shape. A small round or shaped plate was attached to the drawer front as a backing for the handle (see figure).

The pear drop handle was popular in the William and Mary period, often of an acorn shape, but in the early 18th century handles were usually boat-shaped, with a variety of back plates (see figure) culminating in the elaborate pierced back plates of the Chippendale period (see figure).

In the 18th century the brass handles were fixed by nuts and bolts.

In the early 19th century the boat-shaped handle was used in a simple fashion without a back plate, or else a plain wooden knob was fitted.

Harewood This was sycamore, stained greenish-grey and used for bandings and veneers in the late 17th and 18th centuries. It was also known as silverwood.

Hickory This is an indigenous tree of North America. The wood is strong, tough and elastic, making it useful for bent parts where thinness and strength are required, such as the bent parts of Windsor chairs. It is pale red in colour.

Highboy An American high chest-of-drawers; see *Chest of drawers*

High Wycombe This town in Buckinghamshire has been the centre of the Windsor chair industry in England since the 18th century. In the early days chairs were made up in primitive workshops, from parts made by bodgers (see *Bodgers*) in the nearby beech woods of the Chilterns. Gradually the Windsor chair became mass produced in local factories, making High Wycombe one of the first areas to mass produce furniture.

With the introduction of steam power in the 1860s some of the most laborious work was gradually made easier, the circular saw being used to convert timber into planks, although the sawpit was used for a long time for larger planks.

The gradual introduction of more machinery speeded up production. The seat-boring machine, for example, could bore the 60–70 holes needed for a seat that was to be caned in seconds, instead of the lengthy hand-boring method used formerly.

The earliest chair factory

Samuel Treacher had established the first chair factory in High Wycombe with Thomas Widgington by the early years of the 19th century. During this century the number of factories grew to about a hundred, turning out 4,700 chairs a day. Chairs and chair parts left High Wycombe for all parts of the country in horse-drawn waggons, before the coming of the railways. They left for London, 30 miles away, in the late evening, in a waggon train of 30–40 waggons loaded with chairs, on a round trip that would take certainly not less than 36 hours.

From 1801–1960 it has been estimated that High Wycombe produced more chairs than all the London manufacturers put together. Chair catalogues of the second half of the 19th century contained over 140 different chair designs. Travellers from High Wycombe firms sold their goods all over Europe and America. Firms were not only producing Windsor chairs, but many other varieties, including the famous Wycombe lath-backs.

Many of the High Wycombe firms well known today, such as Ercol and G. Gomme Ltd, producers of G-Plan furniture, branched out into many other types of furniture production.

High Wycombe has a unique Chair Museum, which houses a large collection of Windsor chairs, with much information as to how they were made, and the tools used, including a reconstruction of a bodger's hut and a framer's workshop.

(See also *Windsor chair,* in *Chair* section.)

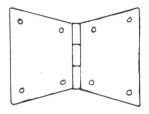
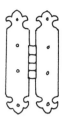

Tudor and Jacobean hinges; on the right is the H-hinge (16th and 17th centuries)

Hoof foot, used on cabriole legs (late 17th and early 18th centuries)

Hinge Most of the early Tudor and Jacobean hinges were of a simple shape in wrought iron. A type extensively used on cupboards of the 16th and 17th centuries was the H-hinge (see figure). All hinges were held in position at this time by handwrought nails.

Holly (*Ilex aquifolium*) A hard wood, greyish-white, among the lightest of all woods, so chiefly used in inlay work to give a contrasting colour. It was sometimes stained to look like ebony.

Hoof foot A foot used on cabriole legs at the end of the 17th and early 18th century (see figure).

Hornbeam (*Carpinus betulus*) A yellowish-white wood, occasionally used for inlay work and turnery and, like the holly, sometimes stained black to look like ebony.

Hutch
See *Cupboard*

Hutchier A carpenter who made shelved cupboards and hutches in the Middle Ages.

Inlay Inlaid work was not common in country furniture. This form of decoration was not used to any great extent until Elizabethan times, and then the inlay work was of a much coarser type than that known a hundred years later, when fine veneers were used in marquetry, in cabinet makers' work.

Small pieces of cherry, ash, beech, yew, holly, bog oak, pear, poplar and sycamore were inserted into the solid wood, usually in geometrical or floral patterns, in many country pieces. The outlines of these patterns were first drawn on the wood surface to be decorated, and the small pieces of contrasting woods fitted about 3 mm ($\frac{1}{8}$ in) into them.

One type of popular chest covered with inlay decoration representing buildings said to be Henry VIII's Palace of Nonsuch in Surrey, are known as 'Nonsuch' chests. It is most probable that these were imported or made by foreign craftsmen.

Inverted cup turning This was a form of turning, sometimes known as a trumpet turning, characteristic of the William and Mary period; it appeared on table legs and the legs of high chests and lowboys (see figure).

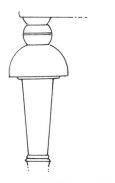

Inverted cup turning (William and Mary)

Jacobean A term applicable to the period of the reign of James I (1603–25) but sometimes extended to cover most of the 17th century, the furniture styles varying little throughout the century in regard to country-made furniture, although there were greater changes in fashionable styles in the cabinet maker's furniture of the latter half of the 17th century.

Jacobean furniture is of a more restrained style than that of the preceding period, with less emphasis on carving and more on turning as a form of decoration. An increasing variety of furniture pieces was produced, especially storage items, such as the chest of drawers, and of lighter, more movable forms of furniture, such as the gate-leg table. The number of chairs, especially side or single chairs, was greatly increased in this period.

JOINER

These craftsmen, who had been organized into Guilds since the 13th century, came to prominence in the 15th century when panelled framing was introduced into England from the Low countries. By the time the more settled conditions of 16th century Tudor England were reached, and changes in the countryside had brought more wealth to the land, most furniture was made by joiners. A change from mainly arable farming to sheep farming had brought new wealth through the wool trade to many farmers and merchants. They all enjoyed higher living standards in their homes, with a greater variety of furniture especially furniture of a more permanent type than that made by carpenters, particularly items in which to store their increased possessions.

This resulted in the joiner becoming a class of woodworker separated from the carpenter (see *Carpenter*), who continued to make the framework of buildings and the simple furniture of plank and trestle construction, leaving the joiner to make most of the furniture and interior fittings of a house from the time of Queen Elizabeth I onwards.

A joiner was an expert in the art of making framing and panelling which produced furniture that did not split or warp but in which the panels could move freely in the frames during changes caused by weather or age; the panelling was therefore under no strain which gave it a much longer life. The frames of horizontal rails and vertical stiles were joined with more refined mortise and tenon joints (see *Joint*) than those used by earlier carpenters, grooved round the inner edges to hold the panels. These had their edges tapered to fit into them. This was a revolution in furniture making and articles constructed in this way were called joined or joint furniture. They were lighter and easier to move than those made by the heavy plank construction used by the carpenters.

The joiners used this method to make panelling for walls, doors, bedheads, settles, chairs, stools and chests. While much of their work was marred by excessive decoration in Elizabethan times, by the 17th century the furniture produced by Jacobean craftsmen became much more restrained. Styles were produced which continued to be made in country districts for the next two centuries and still look well in country homes today.

Later development and specialization One of the items of furniture made by the joiner which grew in popularity in the 17th century was the chest of drawers. The earliest drawers had the fronts nailed to the sides, which had grooves cut in them, so that they could slide on runners fixed to the sides of the chest, a type of drawer that has been revived in the 20th century. By 1650 joiners were making drawers joined at the sides by dovetails, at first rather large and crude, becoming smaller and neater in size by the end of the century (see *Chest of drawers; Drawers; Dovetail*).

In the 18th century there was a further division of the joiner's work between the joiner who made chairs alone, and the joiner who made the wooden frames for beds, and the

framework for settees and those chairs that were eventually covered with material by upholsterers, such as wing armchairs.

By the late 17th and 18th century the cabinet makers took over the making of the fashionable veneered furniture in walnut, and the later mahogany furniture where the construction of the pieces was not so obvious as in the earlier oak construction. They were more concerned with design and effect than the earlier joiners, who concentrated on sound construction and fitness for purpose above everything else; this was an approach to furniture making revived by William Morris and his followers at the end of the 19th century and continued by the best of 20th century furniture makers.

Joint The principal joints used by joiners in the making of country furniture are those that have been in use from the 17th century onwards.

Dovetail This joint used for the construction of drawers is described and illustrated under *Dovetail*.

Mortise and tenon This was the principal joint used in the construction of panels to join the rails and stiles of the framework. The *mortise* was a cavity, usually rectangular in shape into which the protruding *tenon* fitted to form a tight joint (see figure). Until the use of

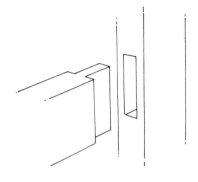

Mortise and tenon joint

glue, a wooden dowel or peg was fitted through the two joined parts for extra strength.

Tongued and grooved This was the joint used to join two pieces of wood side by side (see figure).
(See also *Mitre*.)

Juniper (*Juniperus communis*) This rich brown wood was used for small tables and chests, and for small carvings, as it was rarely available in large widths.

Kas
See *Cupboard*

Laburnum (*Laburnum anagyroides*) A hard, yellowish wood with brown streaks. It was used for inlay work and veneering. In the late 17th century, the branches cut transversely produced the markings known as 'oyster shell'.

Lathe-turning
See *Turner; Tools*

Lime (*Tilia vulgaris*) A creamy white wood, used for carving and turnery, an easily-worked but not a durable wood.

Limed oak Oak pickled with lime, which is then brushed off, leaving some to remain in the grain. The surface is then left unpolished.

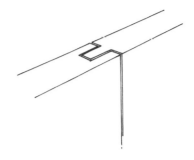

Tongued and grooved joint

Linenfold A form of carving introduced into England at the end of the 15th century. It was used on wall panelling and chests (see *Chest*) and was a popular decoration in the 16th century. The illustration is of linenfold panelling from the Neptune Inn, Ipswich, now in Ipswich Museum, which has a carved foliated frieze with grotesque heads carved on it (see photograph).
(See also *Carver and Carving*.)

Lopers These are sliding pieces of wood which pull out from the framework of a bureau to support the desk front when it is lowered.

Lowboy An American table with drawers.
(See *Chest of drawers*.)

Lozenge A fairly common form of carving for chests and chair backs, in the form of a diamond chape, which appears in the 16th and 17th centuries (see figure).

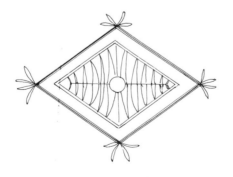

Lozenge carving

Linenfold carving with foliated frieze (16th century)   *Ipswich Museum*

Lunette carving
1 Simple repeat band of semi-circles   2 Incurving lunettes
3 Intersecting lunettes

Lunette A repeat band of semi-circles carved on early 17th century furniture, found on domestic and church woodwork (see figure). Incurving and interlaced lunettes have been found to be a popular design in the south-western counties of England, chiefly found on the rails of chests and chair backs.

Maple (*Acer saccharum*) Extensively used in American country furniture. The hard varieties are almost white, the softer maples give a light-yellowish brown wood. It can be polished very smooth and is used for cabinet making and ornamental veneering.

Medieval A term which covers the 12th to 15th centuries. Also called the Middle Ages. The period comes to an end in Tudor times with changes in religion, architecture and the prosperity and increased security of the country.

Medullary rays These are the lines that radiate outwards from the heart of a tree – the medulla – and cut across the annular rings. They are most strongly marked in oak and beech. Timber which has been quartered then sawn towards the inside cuts, following the medullary rays, shows the grain to the best advantage; this also gives planks of greater hardness and durability, which are less likely to warp.
(See also *Sawyer*.)

Mitre A joint employed by joiners to unite two mouldings framing a panel, at an angle of 45° (see figure). Used by skilled joiners in the 16th century.

Morris, William (1834–96)
In the second half of the 19th century, William Morris led a revolt against the ugliness of the industrial age. Together with some of his friends in 1861 he founded the firm of Morris & Co. in order to revive the craftsmanship of handmade pieces and make them available to

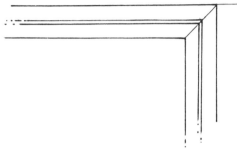

Mitred joint uniting two mouldings
(16th century)

back and seat, decorated with bobbin-turning on rails and stretchers. By 1866 this had become very popular in America, where it was known as the 'Morris chair'. Again the chair was adapted from a Sussex design.

The ideals of William Morris were later continued and interpreted to even better effect by the Cotswold School of designers, his own firm never really producing the simple furniture he hoped for in the quantities he visualized, to compete with the machine produced furniture of the age. His ideas were however to influence some of the best designers of the 20th century.

The woven fabrics and printed wallpapers also produced by his firm achieved a standard of excellence which is recognized in their continuing popularity today.
(See also *Cotswold School*.)

Mortise The cavity, usually rectangular in shape, into which the protruding tenon fits, to join the stiles and rails of panel framing.
(See also *Joint*.)

MOULDING

Mouldings are the shaped edges of a panel frame, a lid of a chest or a table top. The earliest

the masses. His motto was 'Have nothing in your house that you do not know to be useful or believe to be beautiful'.

The furniture produced by the firm was made in oak and beech and was designed by Ford Madox Brown and Philip Webb, among others. The Sussex chair (see page 145), and also *Chair* section) was one of their most successful products. Based on a traditional design, with turned parts and rush seat, it was made of beech and stained dark green, in marked contrast to most Victorian chairs being mass produced at the time.

From about 1866 the firm made an armchair with an adjustable back, upholstered arms,

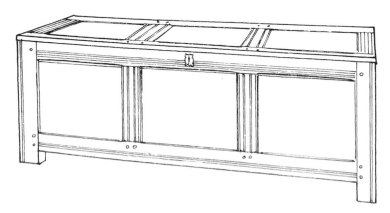

Panelled chest with plain stiles and moulding on top rail, no mitred corners necessary

mouldings were carved out of the solid wood on furniture of the 15th and 16th centuries. *Scratched* mouldings on the edges of frames around panels were not always continuous in early examples, but died out on the surface, leaving a plain square edge where the uprights butted against the rails. In the 17th century the mouldings were of the *continuous run* variety, and mitred at the corners. Less experienced craftsmen continued to stop the moulding before the corner was reached.

The scratch-stock (see under *Tools*) was in early use, but often the mouldings were cut or scratched with gouge or chisels of different shapes. Often on chest panels the mouldings were only on the rails and were mortised to plain stiles, no mitred corners then being necessary (see figure). Unlike the later moulding plane, the scratch-stock could be used around corners and curves, especially in the 18th century on walnut and mahogany.

Applied mouldings When more accurate geometrical shapes were wanted to decorate chests and the newly important chests of drawers in the 17th century, applied mouldings were used. The strips of oak made separately to the carcase could be more accurately cut and mitred at the corners in this way. They were then fitted, glued and bradded into position in a great variety of geometrical designs. Turned mouldings were also used in the same way.

Bead A bead was a type of small semi-circular moulding on 18th century furniture, sometimes resembling a string of beads.

Cock bead This was a projecting moulding consisting of small half round sections, usually applied to drawer fronts in the latter half of the 18th century.

Ogee moulding An ogee moulding was one having an S-shaped profile.

Mule chest
See *Chest; Chest of drawers*

Nonsuch chest
See *Chest; Inlay*

Oak (*Quercus pedunculata*) The oak occurs everywhere in temperate zones in many varieties. It is a coarse-textured hardwood, very durable and strong. Pale yellow in colour, though varying from one district to another, it attains the rich dark colour of antique furniture only with age and polishing. The quality of the oak varies with the district in which it grows. Generally oak from rich soil is easier to work, probably because it has grown more quickly, but from poor soil it is usually hard and tough. Oak is difficult to work and was used in so much early furniture partly because it was easy to split with a wedge.

Onion foot A foot used on 17th century furniture, also known as a ball foot.

'Oyster shell'
See *Laburnum*

Palmated A carving on a chest or chair back which is in the shape of a palm leaf or an acanthus leaf, often within an arcaded panel.

Panels and panelling
See *Joiner; Linenfold*

Pear (*Pyrus communis*) A common hard fruitwood, pink to yellowish-white in colour. Used for carving and inlay.

Pediment An 18th century triangular top found in a bookcase, cupboard or cabinet. It was not much used in country work.

Pendant A hanging knob or turned finial used at the end of the 17th century, which indicated where a leg or support would have been in an earlier style; for example, the columns at the front of a court cupboard, or the underframing of a William and Mary side table or tallboy, when six legs were reduced to four.

Sussex chair, produced by Morris & Co. (late 19th century)
Victoria and Albert Museum

Pine A general term for various coniferous trees in Britain, Europe and America. It is also known as deal. The Scots Pine is extensively used in Scotland for country furniture.

Plane Another name for the sycamore, *Acer pseudoplatanus*, a very white, tough, hardwood, used for painted chairs.

Plate rack Plate racks are often fixtures in country homes, often in an alcove. Hanging sets of shelves for the display of plates are found, usually with a guard rail to stop the dishes falling off. In East Anglia and the north these are still known as delft-racks. Plate racks are often made to match the bottom half of a dresser (see *Dresser*), but are either hanging or free standing on the dresser.

Plum A hard fruitwood, yellow or reddish brown, used for inlay and turned parts.

Pollard oak An oak tree that has been polled *ie*, the top has been cut off and the growth arrested, which gives a dark brown wood with a wavy grain.

Poplar (*Populus nigra,* black poplar; *P. alba,* white poplar) A native British tree, giving a softwood, pale yellow, used for interior parts of furniture, wall panelling and decorative inlay.

Pot board The bottom open shelf of a court or livery cupboard, or dresser.

Press
See *Cupboard*

Quartered oak Oak from a log that has been quartered, and the planks cut from each quarter parallel to the medullary rays (see *Medullary rays*).

Quatrefoil A Gothic decoration made up of four leaves (see figure).

'Queen Anne' Furniture in this style is of the period of the reign of Queen Anne (1702–14), but is used to cover much early 18th century furniture. The period is characterized by walnut and veneered furniture made by cabinet makers, with the cabriole leg and simple graceful splats on chair backs.

Rail The horizontal member of the frame of panelled furniture, or of the back of a chair.

Renaissance The revival of classical forms of ancient Greece and Rome that took place in Italy in the 15th century, influencing architecture and furniture, reached England in the 16th century. Its effect was seen in the carvings used on Tudor furniture in Romayne panels (see figure), acanthus leaves and columns. These never appeared in the pure classical form of the European Renaissance, however, but were mixed with Gothic designs.

Restoration The term applied to the style of furniture of the period following the Restoration of Charles II to the throne in 1660. Continental craftsmen and ideas introduced new methods of construction and design to fashionable furniture in towns. This is particularly seen in the tall chairs with intricate carving and caned seats and backs, and in the

Quatrefoil carving

Romayne panel

Rosette carving, found on both
English and American furniture
(16th and 17th centuries)

Sausage turning, often found on American
furniture (17th century)

elaborate cabinets with veneered fronts.
Country furniture was little affected by these
changes.

Ring turning
See *Ball and ring turning*

Romayne A carving of a head or profile
surrounded by a roundel or circular motif,
introduced from the continent in the reign of
Henry VIII and used to decorate panelled
furniture. Sometimes the head may have been a
likeness of the owner for whom the furniture
was made, sometimes a mythological Roman
head within a wreath.

Rope carving A form of carving along the
rails of chests and chairs in the 17th century
which looks like a coil of rope (see figure). It

Rope carving (17th century)

appears in many areas but was especially
popular in Dorset.

Rosette A decorative carving on chests and
chair backs of the 16th and 17th centuries that
appears on both English and American
furniture, and which may represent the Tudor
rose, or even a sunflower (see figure).

Roundel A circular ornamental carving.

Rugs
See *Carpets and other floor coverings*

Runners This is the name sometimes given to
the curved rockers at the bottom of a rocking
chair.

Sausage turning An elongated form of ball
turning, popular on 17th century American
furniture (see figure).

147

SAWYER

Before mechanization the pit sawyer felled the larger trees and sawed them into planks in a saw-pit. Before this was done the bark was stripped from the trunk with a barking iron. It was necessary for sawyers to work in pairs, one above ground and the other in the pit, the lower man having by far the worst of the bargain. They usually kept to the same pair, as it was necessary for them to know each other's stroke for the sawing to proceed smoothly. The second sawyer dug the pit, which was 1.80 m wide, 3 m long and about 1.60 m deep (6 ft wide, 10 ft long and around 5½ ft deep). The senior partner's main job was to look after the large saw they used, which measured 2 m (7 ft) and was usually his property, and to purchase and prepare the timber for sawing.

A stout framework on which to rest the trees to be sawn had to be built before the actual sawing commenced. The timber to be cut was rolled on to the frame and secured by iron dogs or spikes. The line to be sawed along was marked by a cord rubbed in chalk held taut along the trunk. The top pit sawyer guided and pushed the saw downwards, while the man in the pit, who could see little of what was happening, and often had to work by candle-light, pushed the saw back up to him, being showered by sawdust at the same time. Naturally this was one of the jobs where mechanization came first in the woodyard and where it was most welcome.

When the planks left the sawpit and were sent to the workshops, they were marked out and held rigid on a bench with iron holdfasts, and sawn into shape with a large frame saw. This type of saw had various names, such as the 'up-and-down' saw, 'the dancing Betty' and the 'Jesus Christ' saw, taking its name from the up-and-down movement, a bowing or re-verential action, of the man using it.

The tree-felling season Trees are felled in the autumn or winter, when the wood is as dry as possible and the sap is dormant, but not

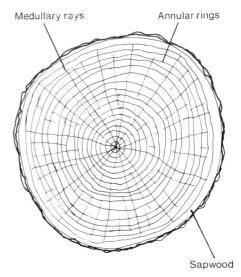

Cross section of tree, showing annular rings and medullary rays

during very cold weather when the wood will be too brittle. In winter there is the least amount of moisture in the tree and the seasoning time will be shortened. Shrinkage and loss of weight will be less. After the bark is removed the trunks are ready to be converted into planks. How this is done gives different results, some methods showing more of the grain of the wood than others.

A section through a trunk (see figure) shows why this is so. The annular rings are formed inside the bark during the summer months of growth, and each shows how much a tree has grown in a year. It is these rings that give the grain to a piece of wood, but only show when the wood is cut across the medullary rays which convey moisture from the outer sapwood to the inner part of the tree.

Methods of sawing Originally the trunks were sawn in layers (see figure), producing planks that diminished in width the further they were cut from the centre. The wood thus produced was plain and uninteresting, but this is the most economical method of conversion, and still used for softwoods where the appearance of the grain is not important.

The later method, used for oak, was to quarter the trunk lengthwise and saw each quarter towards the centre. The planks sawn in this way follow the medullary rays and produce the much desired silvered or figured grained oak. Not only was this quarter-sawn oak or 'wainscot' more beautiful, it was stronger, more durable and less likely to warp.

The amount of silver-grained oak produced varied according to how the wood was cut. Four methods are shown (see figure):

A When planks were sawn in this way there was quite a bit of wood wasted, but the planks would show the most silver-grained wood.

B This method is less wasteful, but gives fewer planks of grained wood.

C This method is less wasteful still but gives even less grained wood.

D This method is used for thicker planks, but gives only 1 and 2 which would show silver grain.

(See also *Seasoning*.)

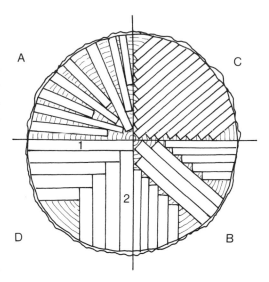

Four methods of sawing, producing varying amounts of silver-grained wood

Schrank
See *Cupboard*

SCOTTISH FURNITURE

The country furniture of Scotland is to a large extent a reflection of the varying landscape of the country. It changes from the extreme north, from Caithness and Sunderland, where many of the influences are Scandinavian, to the south where English influences penetrated the farthest; from the Western Isles and coast where trees are scarce to the eastern coast, where continental influences brought the best quality furniture styles and the highest craftsmanship is found.

Chairs, stools and settles These influences are shown in the caquetoire chairs (see *Chair* section) that are found there in the same style as French chairs, at a time when the Scottish and French crowns were close. They have high class carving, which can also be seen in carving on stonework in Scotland, showing that any lack of carving in Scottish furniture is due more to a shortage of oak trees than to a lack of artistic ability and craftsmanship

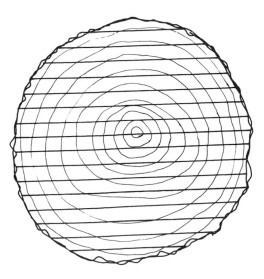

'Through and through' planking

The chair from Caithness (see figure) is believed to show Scandinavian influences in the shape of the arms and rake of the back. Often the back uprights and arms are in one piece bent to shape, or are made from one piece of wood with a natural right angle. In the case of the single chairs the back upright and seat rail are made of one piece of bent wood (see figure).

Where trees are scarce in the Western Isles and coast, much of the early furniture was made from driftwood, such as the armchair illustrated, from Lewis (see figure).

Three-legged stools were also made from driftwood or bogwood where no other wood was available.

From Inverness and Ross-shire comes a stickback chair of the same type as the Cardiganshire chair from Wales, thought to be an early variety of Windsor chair (see figure). These chairs are often made of several different woods, as are the later Windsor chairs. The legs and back sticks were fixed into the seats by the means of holes burned in the seat.

Many of the chairs are low types, but are not necessarily children's chairs. They were made low for homes with a central peat burning fire, so that the occupant sat below the billowing smoke.

The communal settle, *seise* or *seisach* was especially popular in the Highlands and Islands, varying in style according to the amount of wood available (see page 156).

Regional woods The Scots pine trees provided much of the wood for furniture. Most early Scottish chairs of good quality were inscribed and dated, many made on a marriage. These mostly come from the east coast.

Where wood was very scarce basketwork furniture was used (see *Basketry* and *Cupboard*).

As in English country districts the 18th century Chippendale styles of chairs which were made in mahogany in Perth and Edinburgh, or even imported from London, were copied by local craftsmen in beech and ash,

sometimes from chairs which found their way from the wealthier to poorer homes.

Beds Until the 18th century beds were not common in Highland homes. Mattresses filled with heather sufficed until then. The bed that was the most popular was the box bed, which was often entirely enclosed with doors when enough wood was available.

Chests Every home had several kists or chests for the storage of clothes and meal, which could also do duty as stands for dishes. Dressers were plain and made of pine or driftwood.

Tables The Scottish kitchen table was often long and narrow, so that it did not take up too much room. Occasionally it was found with a small edging round three sides, or all the way round the table top. This was to keep the flour on the table during baking. Sometimes this edging had a small gap, so that surplus flour could be brushed off.
(See also *Settle*.)

Scratch carving The design is formed by a single line scratched on the surface of the wood, principally on 16th and 17th century furniture. It is also known as incised carving.

Seasoning When planks of wood are cut it is necessary for the wood to dry out thoroughly to prevent warping. This is now done in kilns, but originally the planks were either stacked in an airy place – not too windy or sunny – with small blocks between them where the seasoning process could take its time; or they were seasoned in an upright position after being soaked in water, such as a river or stream. Early carpenters thought the water immersion reduced the risk of woodworm and was a more effective method of seasoning.

The rule used to be one year's seasoning for each inch of thickness of the planks. Walter Rose writing in the *Village Carpenter* says that

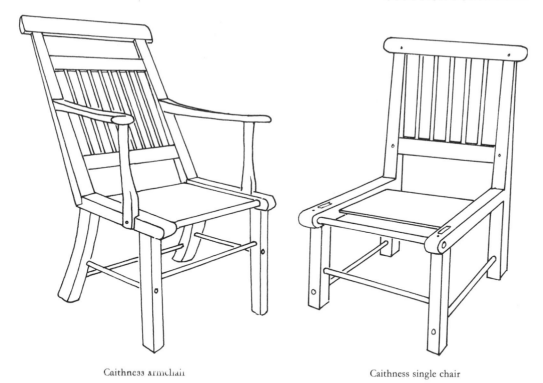

Caithness armchair

Caithness single chair

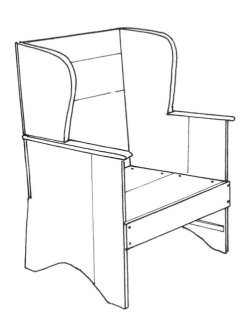

Lewis armchair

Early variety of Windsor chair,
found from Inverness to Ross-shire

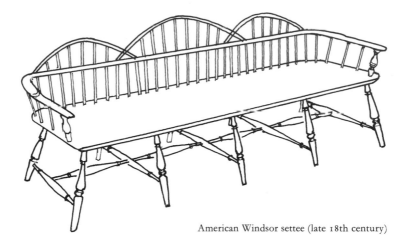

American Windsor settee (late 18th century)

the process of steaming out the sap from sawn planks for quick seasoning leaves the wood reduced in strength and durability, and that heating in a kiln is liable to cause cracks.

Settee This is the term usually applied to an upholstered version of the 17th and 18th century low-backed wooden settle with arms. The transition to the upholstered settee took place in the 18th century, but it is unlikely to have appeared in country homes before the 19th century.

An all-wood settee of Windsor type appeared in the 19th century, not popular in England, which retained the old form of wooden settle for many years in country homes. In America however, Windsor settees were made in a variety of styles, including the bow-back and rod-back, the latter with bamboo type turnings in the back. The settees often give the impression of several chairs joined together with a continuous seat (see figure).

The back of the Chippendale style country settee in oak (see figure) looks like two chairs joined together, but the stretchers and shaped apron are of obvious country workmanship.

SETTLE
This early piece of furniture is often shown

with Gothic decoration in medieval domestic scenes, but although the word 'settle' is found in 16th century inventories, few settles have survived of an earlier date than the 17th century. The settle is strictly a country piece; it never graced fashionable drawing rooms in its early forms, only after it had assumed an upholstered shape and become a settee.

The settle can be seen as a development of both the bench and the chest which took place when increasing standards of comfort were demanded. Like many country pieces it was multi-purpose, doing duty as a combined fireside seat, draught-stopper and storage unit.

Its most usual form comprised a box seat for several persons, framed and panelled, often with a lid forming a locker beneath, and with arms and a high panelled back. Sometimes wings took the place of arms, and the later upholstered wing armchair was a development of this form of seating. It was either fixed to a wall, perhaps in the ingle-nook of a large fireplace, or could be free standing when it was also known as a bank or bink.

Curved settles were popular in many districts, particularly in the south. In Devonshire settles were always semi-circular or crescent shaped. The curved settle illustrated (see figure) was built into its present position about 1880 at a farm in Somerset. It has a storage space under

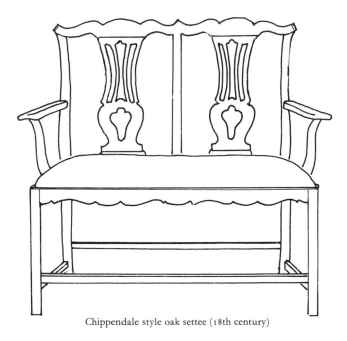

Chippendale style oak settee (18th century)

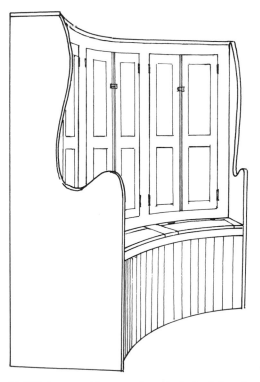

Curved settle with lidded seats and bacon cupboard in the back from Somerset (c.1880)
Museum of English Rural Life, Reading

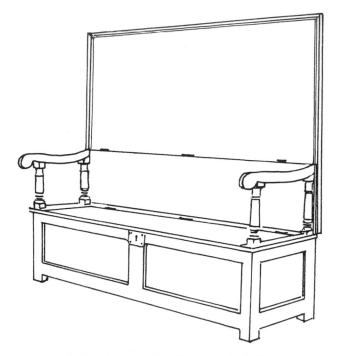

Settle-table (monk's bench) found on both sides
of the Atlantic (c.1650)

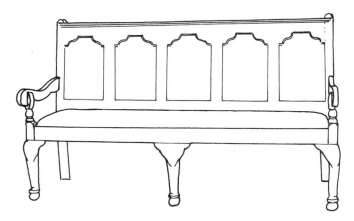

Lancashire oak settle with cabriole legs (c.1760)

the lidded seats and a bacon cupboard in the back, also wing arms.

A piece for many purposes Occasionally, like the box bedstead, the settle acted as a partition to divide a room, instead of a curtain, useful when rooms were few and privacy at a premium. With a mattress on it, it became a bed. Inventories of the early 17th century from northern England mention 'long-settle bed' which suggest that some settles were made purposely for this function.

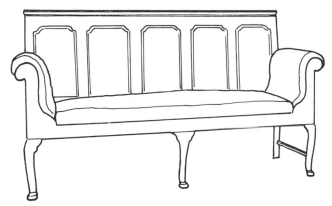

Lancashire Queen Anne settle

There was also a variation, the settle with the back which could be folded over to make a table (see figure). The name 'monk's bench' sometimes given to this piece is a modern term, the settle having more connection with the country inn than the monastery. *The settle-table* was a popular multi-purpose piece made in pine in early American homes.

Early 17th century settles had rope supports for cushions, an early attempt to provide comfort in seating. Holes can often be seen along the rails of the seat into which the ropes were threaded. Many have since been given wooden seats or upholstered ones. By the time of Cromwell settles were found with the same leather seats as the chairs of that period, stuffed with hay or horsehair. At this time a low-backed settle was introduced with open arms at each end. The panelled backs often had a carved back rail along the top. Cabriole legs were sometimes attempted in 18th century settles (see figure).

More upholstery was gradually introduced to make the settle more comfortable, the padding extending from the seats to the arms, on top of the wooden frame, until the settle became the fully upholstered settee (see figure).

Many high-backed settles had storage compartments in the back for sides of bacon. A fine example of a *bacon cupboard* from West Wales, made in elm in the second half of the 18th century is illustrated (see photograph).

Settles with a pen underneath the seat to house a sitting duck or goose are known in

Elm bacon cupboard (West Wales; later 18th century)
National Museum of Wales

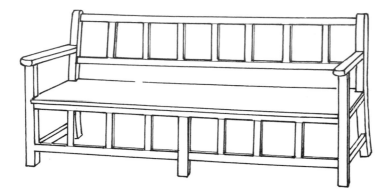

Scottish settle
(seise or sesach)

Cornwall. Due to its versatility the settle retained its popularity in inns and farmhouses long after it had lapsed from favour elsewhere.

It was a very popular seat in the Islands and Highlands of Scotland, where it was known as a *seise* or *seisach* (see *Scottish furniture*). The shape varied according to the timber available in a particular district. It usually had short perpendicular bars forming the back and underframing when wood was scarce, as in the settle shown here (see figure); but in areas where wood was more plentiful it had the usual form of panelled back and box seat, and more unusually, a back formed of turned spindles.

SHAKER FURNITURE

This is furniture produced by a religious sect in America in the second half of the 19th century. 'Shakers' was the name given to members of 'the United Society of Believers in Christ's Second Coming' because of the shaking movements they employed in the course of their religious services.

The sect originated in England and went to America in 1774, under the leadership of Mother Ann Lee, to establish communities all over New England, and later in Ohio, Kentucky and Indiana. In these isolated rural communities they produced a large variety of furniture of the highest quality, design and craftsmanship which is much valued today.

Their religious beliefs of order, harmony and utility made them shun all that was highly decorated and extravagant, and value furniture that was perfectly designed for the purpose for which it was needed, and which was of sound construction, built to last – both attributes that have always been highly regarded in all country furniture.

Though plain and unadorned, except for the staining of the wood, which enhanced its appearance, the beauty of their furniture was in its perfect design. The tripod table illustrated on page 169 has a fragile appearance, yet its perfect balance and sturdiness is a good example of the ideals they put into their work.

Their communal lives led them to favour long trestle-type tables for dining; these were often 6 m (about 20 ft) long, the underframing high under the top to give knee room. They were combined with chairs with very low backs with two curved slats (sometimes even only one) which were comfortable but would not encourage lolling at mealtimes. They fitted easily under the table when not in use, or hung on the strips of peg boards which the Shakers placed high round their walls for hanging articles when not in use, to give a simple uncluttered appearance (see figure overleaf).

The Shaker rocking chairs (see photograph) were perfectly designed for the shape of the human body, and with their ladder backs, finials to the back uprights, and mushroom turnings on the front uprights became very popular. They were also made in small sizes for children.

Shaker
rocking chair
(late 19th
century)
*American Museum
in Britain,
Bath*

Shaker dining chair, made to fit
under table when not in use
(19th century)

They used a variety of local woods such as pine, maple, walnut and fruitwoods. Their chairs had woven seats of hickory splints, cane or rushes. Table tops were made of pine.

Their communal way of living caused the Shakers to design many very plain storage pieces, chests of drawers and cupboards, many of them built into their homes as fixtures.

Shelves These were often fitted into alcoves, but small hanging shelves are found for books and sundry purposes.
(See also *Plate rack*.)

Sideboard A development of the side table used in many farmhouses for serving food, but the term is more usual in town furniture, the farmhouse variety becoming a dresser.

Spanish foot This is sometimes called a paint brush foot (see figure) and is found on 17th century table and chair legs, popular on American furniture.

Spindle A thin turned baluster, used as an upright member of a chair back, or on the guard rails on the plate rack section of a dresser.

Splat The vertical middle support of a chair back, introduced in the reign of Queen Anne, and later ornamented with pierced designs.

Splayed leg The outward sloping leg of a chair or table leg. This was not usual until

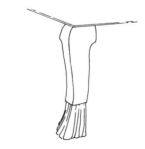

Spanish (or paint brush) foot, popular on
American furniture (17th century)

Split turned ornaments, used in British and American furniture of 17th century

Practically all of them were in oak and made to hang on walls, but many that have a small drawer at the base for small kitchen utensils could stand on a cupboard or dresser.

They often have the appearance of miniature dressers with one or two shelves, a shaped top and carving on the back. The spoons fitted into holes on the narrow shelves.

In the Welsh variety of spoon rack the shelves are of graduated size to form a flight of steps, with holes in each step for the handles.

Standard A medieval term for a large storage chest.

Stickback chair
See *Windsor chair* in the *Chair* section

Stile The outside vertical member of a frame, in joined panel and frame construction.

STOOL
This is a seat for one person, without arms or back, which together with the bench, was the most common form of seating until chairs came into more general use in Tudor times.

comparatively late in the history of chairs in the late 17th century. American Windsor chairs are characterized by the greater splay of their legs in comparison with English Windsors. This is also more apparent in small American tables than in English versions.

Split turned ornaments (Bobbins, balusters and bosses)
These were popular in the 17th century on both sides of the Atlantic as a decoration for chests and chests of drawers (see figure). The turnings were split in two after turning, and glued and bradded into position. Egg shapes and square shapes were also applied in the same way. All these were often stained black to look like ebony.

Spoon rack Most spoon racks that can be seen today date from the 18th century, but they were known from the 16th century onwards, and were common articles in country kitchens.

Three-legged stool In its simplest form it consisted of a flat piece of wood, of any shape, in which three legs were inserted, sometimes flush with the upper side of the seat. These legs were firmly fixed by splitting the tops and driving a wedge in each. Such stools include the traditional milking stool and were an ideal form of seating for uneven farmhouse and cottage floors.

It is difficult to date a particular piece as they were not items likely to have been cherished when worn out or not needed. While many stools in oak have survived, country carpenters must have made hundreds of stools in whatever local wood was available, ash, elm, beech, cherry, apple and pear. These are softer, less durable woods, more prone to woodworm, so have long since disappeared. These three-legged stools are still in use today on

STOOL *Three-legged stool*

Oak stool, from
Buckinghamshire (20th century)
*Museum of English
Rural Life, Reading*

Stool from Gloucester
showing carrying hole (20th century)
*Museum of English
Rural Life, Reading*

farms, and two modern examples are shown here (see photographs), one in oak from Buckinghamshire, 43 cm (17 in) high, with a seat 30 cm (11 in) in diameter, and a smaller one from Gloucester with a hole in the centre for easy carrying. The latter has plainly turned legs, while the legs of the first example are irregularly faced in a series of planed surfaces.

Boarded stool Made by carpenters in the 15th and 16th centuries boarded stools of the slab-ended type of construction had their seat supported by two vertical boards, which were splayed outwards and shaped in the manner of Gothic buttresses. The bottom edges were sometimes shaped to give the appearance of feet. Slotted into these were deep apron pieces set just inside the seat edges, and after the early 16th century decorated with carved or pierced ornament (see figure). These boarded stools continued to be made after 1550 but were gradually replaced by joined stools or joint stools.

Joined stools These were made by joiners,

Boarded stool (16th century)

framed with mortise and tenon joints fixed by dowels or pegs without glue. They could be stacked when not in use beneath the long tables, resting on the stretchers, and were often made in sets matching the table (see figure).

Joined stool (late 16th century)

Round low Windsor stool
(19th century)

Diamond-shaped seated Windsor
stool; rare (19th century)

The best Elizabethan joined stools were heavily carved in oak, but by the 17th century stools became lighter and decoration was limited to light carving on the frieze. The four turned legs straddled outwards, joined to deep rails beneath the seat, and to stretcher rails just above floor level, enabling sitters to keep their feet off draughty, rush-covered floors.

A few stools had three legs and a triangular seat. Some are of straight square formation, resembling miniature tables, and were no

doubt used as such as they are today. Cushions have probably always been used in connection with stools, some 17th century models having the seat shaped to take them.

Windsor type stools were extensively made throughout the 19th century, a round topped variety being the most usual (see figure), with well-turned legs and sometimes a handgrip cut in the centre as in many milking stools. A rarer example had a square top, or in the case of the stool illustrated an unusual diamond-shaped seat (see figure), again with well-turned legs and stretchers. These Windsor stools can be seen in the High Wycombe Chair Museum.

An old term for a low stool or foot-stool was a *Cricket* or *Cracket stool*, and a joined stool was frequently mentioned in late 16th and early 17th century inventories, principally in the county of Cheshire, as a *Buffet*.

Occasionally joined stools are found with a lifting lid with a lock, and a box structure in the upper part of the framework. These *box stools* were probably made for children.

Rarer examples of joined stools had a drawer beneath the seat. One from Salisbury, Wiltshire of about 1640 has a drawer which has side runners fixed to the main frame, the sides of the drawer grooved to slide on them in the manner of the drawers in the earliest 17th century chest of drawers.

In the 17th century the *backstool* came into existence, the back legs of a stool were prolonged upwards to form a back rest. This term lasted for 150 years, and only in the 19th century did the backstool become known as a 'single chair'.

The term *coffin stool* for joined stool is not correct for domestic use, but dates from the middle 18th century when pairs of joined stools were used a bier supports in both church and home. These were slightly taller than the normal joined stool.

Strapwork Carving of interlaced ribbon effect or chain pattern, popular at the end of the 16th and early 17th centuries.

Stretcher The horizontal member connecting the legs of chairs or tables; originally necessary to strengthen the legs and as a foot rest to keep feet off floors that were draughty and covered with rushes. When not needed for this purpose the stretcher was still used on chairs, but was moved higher up the leg.

Stretchers are arranged in various patterns, the H-stretcher, the double H, cross or X-shaped (see figures).

H-stretcher

Double H-stretcher

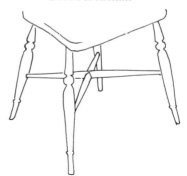

X-stretcher

Cow-horn stretcher

On late 17th century chairs stretchers were often elaborately carved or arched.

The Windsor chair makers in England introduced the *cow-horn* stretcher which was a form of stretcher where the front legs of the chair were braced by a curved bow, from which two spurs link the bow to the back legs, also known as a spur stretcher, or a crinoline stretcher, the shape accomodating the crinoline skirts of the age (see figure, previous page).

In the Charles II and William and Mary period flat stretchers were used, particularly on small tables.

Sunk carving This recessed carving removed the background of the design, leaving the pattern raised. Used in the 17th century.

Sweet chestnut (*Castanea sativa*) This tree gives a light brown wood, sometimes used for panelling in stead of oak, and in the 17th century for tables, chests, chairs, stools and beds.

Sycamore (*Acer pseudoplatanus*) A hard white wood, yellowing with age, used for turned parts, veneers and dairy utensils. Often stained, sometimes black to represent ebony.

TABLE

The earliest tables were of the *trestle* type, with a movable top, resting on trestle supports, referred to in the 15th and 16th centuries as a 'board', from which we get our expressions 'festive board' and 'board and lodging'. These tops were made up of several massive planks held in position by cross-battens on the underside, although the weight of the tops, often 10 cm (4 in) thick, was usually enough to keep them secure. The planks were either tongued and grooved or fixed together with dowels or large wrought iron nails. The trestle supports, listed separately in inventories, were either independent or held in position with one or two cross-rails, which passed through the trestle ends and were fastened on the outside by

oak wedges, supposedly easily removable when the table was taken apart to be stored away. In fact, the size of these carpenter-made tables was such that it must have taken several men to move them.

In the 16th century the trestles became permanent, one at each end resting on a broad base and still connected and strengthened by stretchers. The trestle table shown here (see photograph) is of about 1600 date, and comes from Ipswich Museum, and as was so often the case, the underframing is of oak and top of elm.

In America this type of table, heavily built with X-shaped supports, is known as a *sawbuck* table. The trestle table was a popular style made by the Shakers in America in the 19th century, suitable for the communal type of living they preferred. Their tables, though often 6 m (20 ft) in length, were of a lighter type than the earlier sawbuck tables, the centre cross-rail connecting the two ends was placed high underneath the table top, enabling the diners to sit at the table without their knees being obstructed by the rail.

Framed or joined table In the 16th century the framed or joined table appeared (the table dormant) with a top fixed to the underframing and tenoned into four, six or eight legs, sometimes straight and sometimes turned, the whole made by joiner, turner and carver combined. The legs were joined at the bottom by stretchers, a few inches from the ground, which were mortised into the legs and secured by wooden pegs. These tables are often given the modern name of 'refectory tables' but they have no connection with monasteries, and the name is not contemporary. Tables such as these were made in country districts well into the 19th century.

The draw table Elizabethan examples of both this type of table and the draw table which appeared in the middle of the 16th century had richly carved legs. The underframing also provided a frieze for decoration. The draw

Elm trestle table with underframing of oak (*c*.1600)
Ipswich Museum

Joined oak table (*c.*1650)

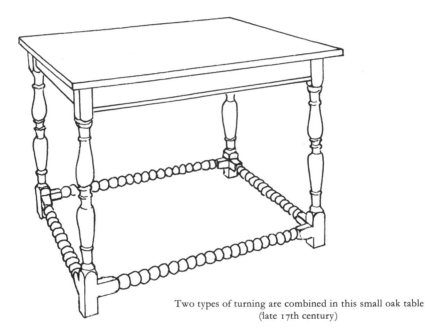

Two types of turning are combined in this small oak table
(late 17th century)

table was capable of extension to double its length by pulling out a pair of draw leaves from under the main table top. The same principle is still used in draw leaf tables today.

17th century developments
In the 17th century the practice of carving the

legs after turning ceased. The heavy bulbous shapes of the Elizabethans gave way to a plain baluster or column shape. When the table top was not fixed to the frame, as was often the case with farmhouse tables, one side could be polished for use as a dining table, and the other side used as a scrubbed working surface. This

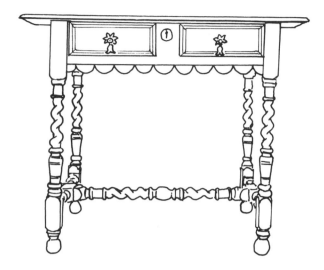

Occasional table with barley sugar turning
and scalloped apron (*c.* 1670)

Country version of fashionable town table
(late 17th century) *Ipswich Museum*

was also the case with earlier trestle tops when underside cross battens were not used; the planks were often joined together with cross pieces at each end instead of underneath (see figure, page 166).

In America when the tops were of pine, the huge trees furnished planks so large that joined planks were unnecessary.

Framed side tables are still found in most Welsh farmhouses. They have carved and shaped friezes, and often the legs are chamfered and united with deep stretchers. These chamfered legs were a style that persisted to a late date in Wales.

Small *occasional* and *side tables*, often with one or two drawers, were in general use by 1625. The small oak table of the second half of the 17th century (see figure, page 166) shows that country craftsmen did not worry about combining two types of turning in one piece; it has vase-turned legs and ball-turned stretchers.

In the slightly later table the barley sugar turning of the period appears on both legs and stretchers, and the table has a drawer and a scalloped apron beneath (see figure, page 167).

A small country-made example (see photograph) from Ipswich Museum illustrates how late 17th century craftsmen attempted copies of the more fashionable town pieces to please their clients. It is in oak with herring bone banding, inlaid into the oak in emulation of walnut veneer cross-banding. The single drawer is still of early construction, with grooves in the side running on side bearers. The baluster legs are joined by cross-stretchers.

Circular tables There were a variety of circular tables of 18th and 19th century date in use in country homes. One was the *cricket* table, a plain round table with three legs, perhaps linked with the old word cricket or cracket, which was often applied to a low stool with three legs, but the term is not contemporary (see *Tavern furniture*).

The oak *tripod* table of the late 18th century

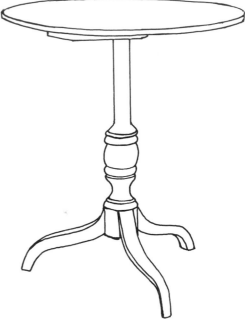

Oak tripod table
(early 19th century)

had a turned central support and three spreading feet (see figure). This was a popular style throughout the 19th century, with a hinged top that folded down against the upright. When brought up into position it became fixed with a spring snap.

The tripod table reached the heights of elegance with the Shaker pedestal tables of the 19th century, which managed to look light and graceful, while being so perfectly balanced and sturdy. The example from the American Museum at Bath is in cherrywood and maple (see photograph).

The Pembroke table Another small table of the same date was the Pembroke table, which had a comparatively long top and short flaps with wooden hinges, which when opened were supported by wooden brackets. It was popular on both sides of the Atlantic (see figure overleaf).

Shaker tripod table in cherrywood and maple (19th century)
American Museum in Britain, Bath

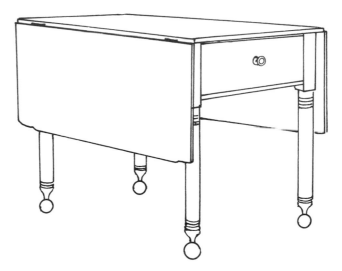

Pembroke table (American; 19th century)

The Sutherland table Its opposite form, a table with a narrow fixed top and very wide flaps, which when opened out were supported on folding out legs, not on brackets, was the Sutherland table. This appeared about 1860 and remained popular for about 50 years.

Gate-leg tables These are the most popular of folding tables, already known in the 16th century. Those in use today are similar in design to those made in the 17th century, when the popularity of this table was at its height. They were made in large numbers here and in America. There are as many as twelve different known designs in England, and the table was made in New England and other American colonies in different woods and with a variety of turned legs.

The most usual form has eight legs, four on each side, two composing the 'gate', framed with top and bottom stretchers (see figure). The top can be round or oval and is composed of three pieces, the side sections being flaps hinged to the rigid middle section on the underside. Hinges on the flaps were small wrought iron ones secured with nails until the introduction of screws in the second half of the 17th century. The two gates swing out to support the flaps, one opening one way and one the other, one of the legs being pivoted to the main framing.

In the 16th century, as living rooms became smaller and furniture more plentiful, it became necessary to produce a table that broke away from the earlier large fixed tables made for spacious dining halls, and which could fold against a wall as a side table when not in use for meals. The gate-leg table filled this need then and has survived because it still fills the need today for a versatile table for a small home.

It may have developed from the triangular three-legged side table with folding top and pivoted supports (see figure).

Later types
A long line of craftsmen introduced both new details of construction as well as personal touches of ornament over the years, culminating in the elaborate mahogany models of the 18th century. Every country craftsman desired to produce his own version of the gate-leg table, in the same way as he would produce

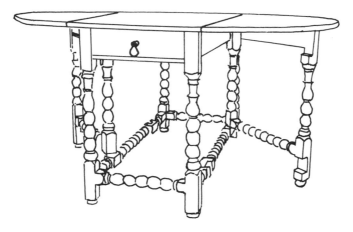

Gate-leg table with ball turning (17th century)

Triangular gate-leg table (*c.*1640)

his individual version of Chippendale chairs.

While the top was usually round or oval it could also be square, oblong or even octagonal. When drawers were fitted they were set in the underframing. Legs and stretchers at first square, were eventually subject to a variety of treatments, such as the early types with urn legs. A small table (see overleaf) shows how Gothic trestle feet persisted.

Later, legs were ball turned, egg-and-reel turned, and in the reign of Charles II, the peak period for gate-leg tables, barley sugar twist turning was usual.

On some types of *Yorkshire tables* the stretchers are splat-form, like the back of a ladder-back chair. These date from 1660–1750. The one illustrated has ball-turned legs (see overleaf). As on side tables, the turning of stretchers did not always match, such was the versatility of designs.

Small gate-leg table with trestle feet (first half 17th century)

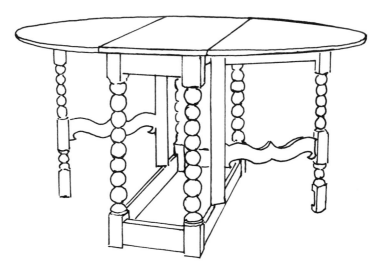

Gate-leg table, Yorkshire type (1660–1750)

A unique American version of a small drop-leaf table, the *butterfly* table, originating in Connecticut, was produced during the 18th century, often in maplewood. This table was made in a variety of sizes throughout New England. It had its leaves supported by brackets shaped like butterfly wings, and splayed legs for greater stability (see figure).

From a simple table with four legs, the gate-leg developed into a type with double gates and twelve turned legs by the reign of Charles II (see figure).

Some very small examples were intended for travelling purposes for use in country inns, where furniture was still scarce. Many of these are made in yew.

American butterfly table (early 18th century)

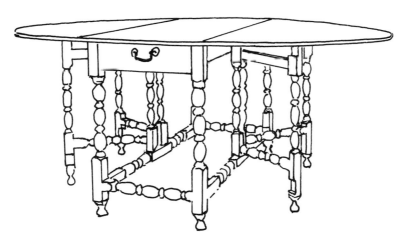

Double-gated and twelve legged table (Charles II)

The small triangular table illustrated (see photograph overleaf) is a country crafted version of a fashionable type. It has one triangular let-down leaf, three turned legs, with one of them hinged as a gate. It is of mid- to late-17th century date.

The turning on the legs of gate-leg tables became more and more intricate, especially when they came to be made by town craftsmen in walnut and mahogany with four to six cabriole legs. The country craftsman continued to make the oak varieties throughout the 18th century. That they were not always of elaborate style even at this date is shown by a primitive example (see figure overleaf), probably made by a local carpenter in the early

Small triangular table (mid to late 17th century)
Ipswich Museum

Primitive gate-leg table (early 18th century)

18th century, with two gates at one end, and the legs not turned but chamfered.

The gate-leg table had a revival in popularity at the end of the 19th century when William Morris preached a return to furniture that was simple and beautiful, but which also fulfilled a utilitarian purpose . . . a role the gate-leg table has fulfilled for four centuries.

Tallboy A tall chest of drawers; see *Chest of drawers*

TAVERN FURNITURE

Some of the best examples of country furniture can be found in the inns and taverns of the countryside. Here high back settles provide draught-free havens from ever-opening doors and trestle tables and benches abound. *Windsor chairs* in all styles are found, the smoker's bow type being especially popular. All these provide hard wearing furniture that will stand up to constant use. It is said that a Windsor chair is so constructed that it can be thrown across a room without it falling apart (see *Windsor chair* in the *Chair* section).

Small tables are found in country inns in all shapes and sizes. In America many small tables are known as *tavern tables*. They were useful for providing a table, quickly and easily, wherever the customer was sitting. They came in many styles, two 18th century types are illustrated. The first, an oval-topped tavern table in walnut, has turned legs, splayed for stability, joined by square stretchers to give strength (see figure overleaf). A rectangular-topped shape, probably made in pine, has a drawer in the underframing. It has vase-turned legs, again joined by square stretchers (see figure).

Small *gate-leg tables* are found in English inns as well as the popular *cricket tables*. A 17th century one (see figure overleaf) has vase-turned legs, joined by plain stretchers.

As well as shelter, rest and food, the

Oval-topped tavern table
(American; 18th century)

Cricket table
(17th century)

Rectangular topped tavern table with drawer
(American; 18th century)

Oak shove ha'penny table (mid-17th century)
Ipswich Museum

furniture of country inns also provided recreation. The oak shovelboard or shove ha'penny table shown here (see photograph) is said to have come from an inn near Newmarket, and is now in Ipswich Museum. It is a joined table of mid-17th century date with four ball and reel-turned legs. It has two drawers with pendant loop iron handles of reversed heart form. The low stretcher, which is worn all round, is especially worn on the left hand side of the playing position, where generations of players have stood and where the game is marked off on the table.

In coaching inns where travellers waited for the next stage or mail coach, the large *tavern clocks* (see *Clock*) of the 18th century were an important accessory to the premises. They were large, weight-driven clocks with wooden dials, usually painted black with gilt figures, and with a short case below.
(See also *Table*.)

Tenon The protruding part of the mortise and tenon joint which was hammered into the mortise cavity, so that the two surfaces of the joined frame were flush. A peg or dowel was inserted through the two parts to hold them firm.
(See also *Joint*.)

Tester The wooden canopy over a four poster bed, sometimes covered with material.

TOOLS

Much of the design and construction of furniture through the ages was influenced by the quality and number of tools available to the craftsman. As the tools themselves improved as each century went by, especially when the 17th century was reached, so did the quality of the items produced. We can only marvel at the work produced by the early woodworkers, working in oak and using only the most primitive tools. It is probable that country craftsmen have always had to work with a few basic tools, many of them of a type in use since the Middle Ages. Most furniture, even in cabinet makers workshops in towns, was made by hand until the end of the 19th century. Although machines for cutting, planing, boring and tenoning were available at the end of the 18th century, it was many years before their use was general. Many early machines still needed human labour to turn handles to work them. Some of the tools used in making furniture until recent times are described below.

Adze A long-handled axe of curved dished form (see figure) used in a chopping action to hollow out the saddle-shaped elm seats of Windsor chairs, and to trim logs when they had been split by beetle and wedge. The adze had a striking head which could be hammered to cut through knots. The cutting edge was at right angles to the curved handle, which was about 70 cm (28 in) long, the blade being about 8 cm (3 in) wide and 23 cm (9 in) long. The marks of the adze can be seen on many pieces of old furniture and on early panelling give an entirely different effect from the smooth finish made by a plane.

Barking iron This was a simple iron tool with a heart-shaped end on a wooden handle (see figure). The bark of the tree was stripped off with this immediately the tree was felled, before the larger branches were cut off. Circles were cut round the tree with a light axe at

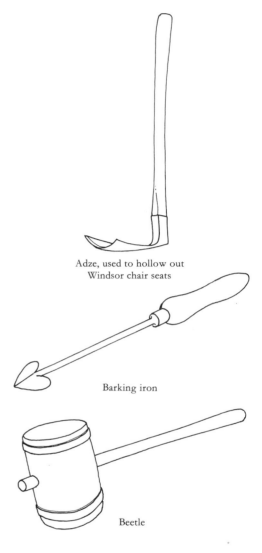

Adze, used to hollow out Windsor chair seats

Barking iron

Beetle

intervals of 60 cm (2 ft). Then one long cut was made the length of the tree, into which the barking iron was inserted, enabling a complete piece of bark to be removed. The bark shells were stacked on end to dry and later could be sent to a tannery.

Beetle This is a form of wooden mallet which was sometimes homemade, a short-handled, barrel-shaped tool, ringed to prevent splitting, and widely used in rural woodwork (see figure). It was used with a wedge to split logs into pieces for chair legs. It is heavier than a carpenter's mallet. The metal safety rings would not always stay in place in the summer, when the wood was dry, so a beetle without rings was called 'a summer beetle'.

Brace and bit A brace which could take a variety of bits to bore holes was known in the 17th century, but the framers who assembled Windsor chairs had a set of braces, each with a different shaped bit for boring the holes in seats, stretchers and spindles. These spoon bits were scoop shaped and would bore a clean hole at any angle using a to-and-fro movement by a half turn (see figure).

Chisel This tool was used by woodcarvers and turners. The bodgers turning Windsor chair parts on their pole-lathes used a V-shaped chisel to cut the bobbin decoration on the legs (see figure).

Cross-cut saw This was used for cutting trunks into 'billets' – roughly formed chair legs – ready to be shaped on a lathe. It cuts both ways and while really designed to be used by two people, it was possible for a man to use it alone. It has unraked and widely set teeth (see figure).

Draw-knife (or draw-shave)
This consists of a narrow blade with a handle at each end, fitted into it at right angles. The workman pulls it towards him to shape a chair leg (see figure).

Frame saw (or bow saw)
This is a saw of great antiquity, called also an 'Up-and-down saw', 'Dancing Betty' and 'Jesus Christ' saw, from the up-and-down and bowing movement of the man using this large saw which is made in various shapes. It has a blade some 75 cm (30 in) long for sawing larger parts, and less than 18 cm (7 in) long in the smaller bow saw for cutting the intricate patterns in the splats of Windsor chair backs.

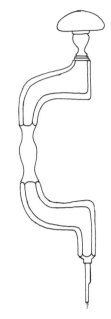

Brace and bit

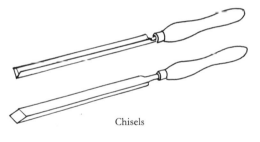

Chisels

Cross-cut saw

Draw-knife

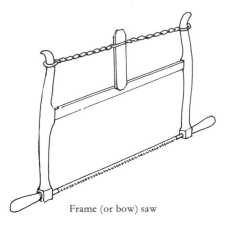

Frame (or bow) saw

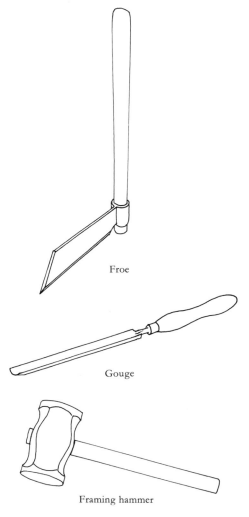

Froe

Gouge

Framing hammer

The blade is tightened by means of the rope and can be adjusted to any angle (see figure).

Froe A metal tool used for cutting billets or roughly shaped chair legs from slender trunks. It has a right-angled handle, and was used in conjunction with a beetle (see figure).

Gouge A carving tool in use since the Middle Ages. It leaves a semi-circular depression (see figure).

Iron dogs (or spikes)
These were used in securing the timbers to be sawn in a saw pit. The wooden long-legged saw-horse used when sawing the trunks into logs was also known by this name. The irons were about 60 cm (2 ft) long with right-angled cross-spikes welded at each end. One cross-spike was driven into the side of the log and the other into the framework over the pit; by which means the trunk was kept rigid in position for sawing.

Hammer The metal framing hammer used by the chair framer for assembling the parts of a Windsor chair (see figure).

Keyhole saw This was a primitive type of saw often used to cut the intricate patterns in the back splats of Windsor chairs (see figure).

Moulding plane This was the tool used for the quickest and cleanest method of making decorative furniture mouldings. Early mould-ing planes often had a hole at the front to take a cord, by which an assistant could pull, while the craftsman could push and guide the plane along the piece of wood to be moulded; the use of the plane on oak was hard work. The disadvantage was that it could not be used on curves and also had to be taken the entire length of the piece of wood being decorated without being stopped. To produce a variety of mouldings a large range of planes had to be used, and this was not possible for a country craftsman and not practicable for a travelling craftsman. These men were more likely to carve their mouldings with gouge and chisel or scratch-stock. The manufacture of moulding planes was a separate trade by the early 18th century.

Pit saw This is the large saw used in saw-pits. It was over 2 m (7 ft) in length, tapering in width from 25 cm (10 in) at the top end, held by the top sawyer, to 7–10 cm (3–4 in) at the bottom, held by the man in the pit. This tapering reduced the weight when the saw was returned to the up position. The handles at each end were detachable. The top handle which guided the saw was called the 'tiller' and the lower one, the 'box'.

Pole-lathe This is a type of lathe that has been in use since Iron Age times for all types of turning. It was the lathe used by the bodgers (see *Bodger*) who made the turned parts of Windsor chairs, and was still in use in factories in High Wycombe in the early 20th century (see figure).

The bed of the pole-lathe consists of two pieces of wood fixed horizontally upon legs, a few inches apart and parallel to each other with a groove between them. Into this groove are wedged the 'poppets', the two heads of the lathe between which the leg is centred for turning. The lathe gets its power from a 3.60 m (12 ft) ash or larch pole firmly fixed to the ground, outside the bodger's hut or workshop. The pole passes through the roof of the hut to the spot above the lathe. Some turners used the living tree as a pole. The end of the pole is joined to the foot treadle by the cord, which is wrapped once or twice around the material to be turned. When the foot treadle is pressed the pole bends and the material turns, to spring back again when the foot is removed. The chisel can only be applied when the material moves forward and the foot is pressed down. There is a photograph of a pole-lathe in operation on page 34.

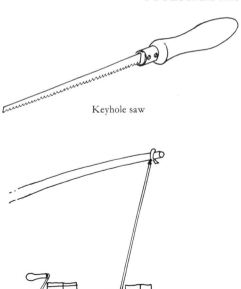

Keyhole saw

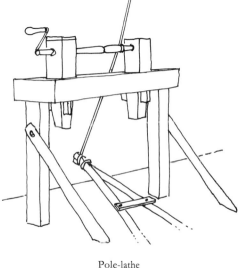

Pole-lathe

Ring dog An appliance used by sawyers for moving heavy logs.

Scratch-stock This tool is still in use where hand work has survived and is used to work mouldings and grooves except where these were made with carving tools. Cutters of various shapes could be fitted into a scratch-stock, which consisted of two pieces of wood screwed or bolted together, with a notch along the bottom (see figure). It could be pressed hard against the edge of the wood as the tool

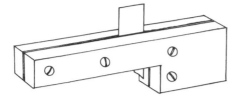

Scratch-stock

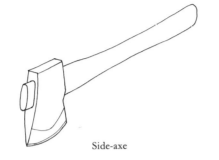

Side-axe

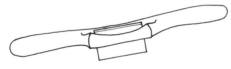

Spokeshave (devil)

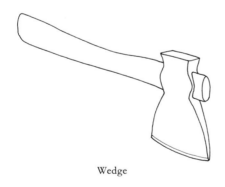

Wedge

was worked backwards and forwards, the cutter scratching or scraping the wood.

Shave horse (or shaving horse) A low bench used by woodworkers for shaping timber. They sit astride it with the piece of wood to be shaved held in a clamp, controlled by the worker's foot. The shaving horse used by chair bodgers had pieces of serrated steel inserted in the clamping blocks to prevent the green wood used in Windsor chair legs suddenly piercing the workman's chest.

Side-axe A small splitting-out axe, used to trim chair legs to a rough shape, before they were further shaped with a draw-knife. It has a handle 15 cm (6 in) long and a blade sharpened on one side only (see figure). It was used mainly for heavy trunks.

Spokeshave A planing tool used to smooth parts of a chair before assembly. There were a variety of these small, two handled tools, including the travisher which had a curved blade, a clearing-off iron to smooth a chair seat and a devil, a scraper with a vertical blade (see figure).

Wedge A splitting-out hatchet with a blade less than 8 cm (3 in) wide, used with a beetle to split logs into pieces, *eg*, for chair legs.

Tracery Pierced carving in Gothic designs often on early food cupboards as a form of ventilation.

Tudor The term applied to the style of furniture and decoration of the period from the beginning of the reign of Henry VII (1485) to the end of the reign of Elizabeth I (1603). The style shows the increase in the wealth and stability of the country, in the increase in the variety of the furniture after the sparsity of the Middle Ages; the greater number of storage pieces for possessions also reflect this. There were many more single chairs, too, during this period as additional seating. There was also an exuberance of carving, especially shown in the bulbous shapes of legs, bedposts and court cupboard supports.

Turkey work This was a knotted wool textile, the technique of which was imitated from imported Turkish carpets. It was extensively used to cover chairs from about 1600 onwards. The flowers in coloured wools are the same as on contemporary English embroidery. Chairs covered with Turkey work are mentioned in farmhouse inventories in Essex of the 17th and 18th centuries.

TURNER

This is one of the earliest types of craftsmen, producing turned objects in ancient Egypt, using a primitive type of pole-lathe (see *Tools*) which was known in Iron Age times, and used in some districts in England until the present century. Turned chairs appear in many medieval illustrations showing that this was one of the earliest chairs, developed from the traditional three-legged stool to become a riot of turned parts in chairs of the 17th century, examples of which are found in Wales, Herefordshire, Lancashire, Cheshire and the West Country. A Welsh example of 1550 date is illustrated on page 72.

The wheel lathe was developed during the 16th century and the turned chair is often known as a 'thrown chair' (see *Turned chair* in the *Chair* section).

The large bulbous turnings of the Elizabethan period on table legs and court cupboard supports were made by gluing four sections to the part to be turned. These were then turned before being carved.

The turners came into their own in the 17th century, when they produced graceful balusters and columns which were no longer carved, and the large variety of turned patterns used in the stretchers and legs of chairs and the gate-leg tables that were so popular at this time (see *Table*). These were allowed to continue and develop during the Commonwealth period when carving was frowned upon by the Puritans. 17th century furniture was largely decorated with turned spindles, pendants and bosses, split in half and glued into place, instead of with carvings (see *Split-turned ornaments*). They were usually stained black.

Bobbin turning was the most popular at this period.

When the Restoration took place the turners were able to add a special device to their lathe to enable it to cut obliquely and produce a greater variety of spirals and twists, especially the barley sugar twist. Before this the turner had only been able to cut shapes at right angles to the work. Where walnut was used for so much town furniture, the country turner often used elm, beech and yew to produce the more delicate turnings required by his clients at this time.

The long experience of turners in country districts enabled them to produce the strongest and lightest of 18th century country chairs, the Windsor chair, without it being necessary for them to produce crude and earlier designs. The Windsor chair appeared as a fully developed design at the end of the 17th century. The turners who made the legs and stretchers of these chairs, working in the beech woods of the Chiltern area of High Wycombe in Buckinghamshire, became known as bodgers.

It was in making these country chairs in the 18th century that turners were kept busy, as there was a decline in the popularity of turning in the fashionable town chairs, until it was made popular again in the Robert Adam period of design after 1760.

(See also *Barley sugar twist; Bobbin turning; Egg-and-reel; Sausage turning; Spindle; Vase turning; Windsor chair*, in the *Chair* section.)

Underframing The framework of a table that supports the top, the framework supporting a chair seat or cabinet.

Upholsterer The 18th century form of this name was 'upholder'. They were the craftsmen who covered chairs and settees with padding, and who also made the hangings and covers for beds, and curtains.

Upright The vertical members of a chair back.

Vase turning

Vase turning A common 17th century turning in the shape of a vase (see figure).

Veneering Thin sheets of wood laid on a base of stronger wood. This was introduced into England at the end of the 17th century by continental craftsmen, necessitating new methods of construction for furniture, and new designs which made the construction less obvious than in the furniture produced during the preceding centuries.

VICTORIAN

This is the term applied to furniture of the reign of Queen Victoria (1837–1901) but this long period of history actually covers many different styles. It is characterized by the increase in the amount of furniture in homes, due to the greater prosperity brought about by the industrial revolution. The gradual mechanization of woodworking techniques resulted in cheaper and more plentiful supplies of furniture to all homes, including country homes. The newly prosperous industrialists created an extra demand for furniture, much as happened with the increased prosperity of the merchant classes in the reign of Elizabeth I, and as in the 16th century, the demand was for ornate designs with elaborate carving.

Romantic revival The early years of Queen Victoria's reign showed a continuation of late 18th century styles, but gradually a more elaborate carving of romantic patterns became popular. This was fostered by the popularity of such writers as Sir Walter Scott, and the name of his Scottish home – Abbotsford – was given to some of the more elaborately carved furniture. Woodcarving became a popular pastime for amateurs as well as professional carvers, and many plain pieces of early oak furniture suffered in this way.

In the countryside the work of the village carpenters was gradually ousted by the cheaper furniture coming from the towns. One exception was in the continuous growth and great popularity of the Windsor chair, in production throughout the 19th century. (See also William *Morris* and *Cotswold School*.)

Wainscot This comes from the Dutch 'wagenschott oak', the oak sawn for the shafts of a wagon, which was quarter sawn to give the strength needed. The oak cut in this fashion was seen to be beautifully marked and was used for panelling. The Dutch craftsmen who worked in England brought this word wagenschott or wainscot to us, and it came to be given to all oak, and the panelling from which it was made.

Walnut (*Juglans regia*) The serious cultivation of this tree began in the reign of Elizabeth I, and the trees came to maturity in the reign of Charles II, when walnut furniture became fashionable. The brown wood develops beautiful markings of darker streaks, when it is known as 'black grain' much sought after for veneers. When English walnut became scarce imported walnut was used by town craftsmen, the native variety still being used by country woodworkers, but with increasing rarity owing to diminishing supplies. Although the wood is liable to attack by woodworm, it does not warp easily and is used for the best gun stocks.

Wardrobe A modern term for a press cupboard. See *Cupboard*.

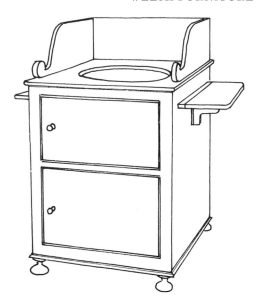

Wash hand stand
(19th century)

Wash hand stands This dates from the middle of the 18th century; it was probably not common in country homes until the 19th. A small table with a bowl on it served most purposes. Wash hand stands were made in rectangular forms and in three-legged triangular versions that would fit into a corner. Some had a hole in the top to take a bowl. Many cheap versions in beech or deal were painted on top to resemble the marble tops of more expensive types (see figure).

WELSH FURNITURE

Until the 18th century the furniture of most Welsh farmhouses and cottages was made by local craftsmen from the wood of the oak, ash or elm growing at hand. It was generally plain and severe in form, but where there was carving or turning it was of a high quality. While some ideas and designs from England may have found their way back to Wales through Welshmen visiting the Tudor and Stuart courts, there were few English visitors to Wales until Europe was closed to travellers by the Napoleonic Wars, when they turned to

Wales for journeys in search of new experiences. Even within Wales itself geographical features made contact between the north and south of the country difficult until well into the 19th century, all of which resulted in certain articles of furniture developing along individual lines in different areas.

The remoteness of country areas caused styles to linger longer than they did in towns, but this also applies to English country furniture and the same problems of dating pieces apply. As L. Twiston-Davies and H. J. Lloyd-Johnes point out when discussing Welsh chairs in their book *Welsh Furniture*: 'The collector of Welsh chairs must therefore be satisfied with the excellence of workmanship, and should not attach too much importance to originality of design or accuracy of date'.

The Welsh dresser The differences in designs in various parts of Wales is shown when we look at the most popular of pieces, the Welsh dressers. Dressers made in North Wales usually have cupboards in the lower half.

A typical early 18th century example would

Oak dresser from Swansea valley (Welsh; early 19th century)
National Museum of Wales

have a foliated frieze and fielded and shaped door panels. Illustrated is an early 19th century dresser (see photograph) from the Swansea Valley in oak, with a shaped cornice and sides, the lower portion under the drawers left open and fitted with an apron piece, as was more usual in the south. The north of Wales had more contact with the northern counties of England and with Ireland than it did with south Wales. The population became more prosperous and thus their furniture was more richly ornamented, carved and varied in style.

Custom-built pieces That Welsh craftsmen were capable of producing fine items to order for special customers is shown by many 18th and 19th century pieces of good quality in mahogany and walnut, such as bureaux, chairs, tall-boys, long case clocks, side tables and dining tables, and the fine large bookcases built into many Welsh country houses by local joiners. An example of the work of one of the

Oak bureau cabinet (Welsh; 1805)
National Museum of Wales

few known names of furniture makers is the bureau cabinet illustrated. This is made in oak, inlaid with chequer patterns and was made in 1805 by William Williams, cabinet maker of Llandovery in Carmarthenshire.

Cupboards Introduced into Wales in the 16th century the court cupboard was popular there longer than anywhere else. It is rarely found in the west of the country where, as in the south-west, the furniture is of a plain variety. Once introduced the *cwpwrdd deuddarn* – the two-piece cupboard – developed along characteristic lines, with carved uprights and lower rail, until by the middle of the 17th century an extra canopy and shelf was added, and the *cwpwrdd tridarn* – the three-piece cupboard – was born, a uniquely Welsh piece of furniture.

Another piece of furniture unique to Wales is the '*y coffer bach*', a small edition of a mule chest used as a Bible box.

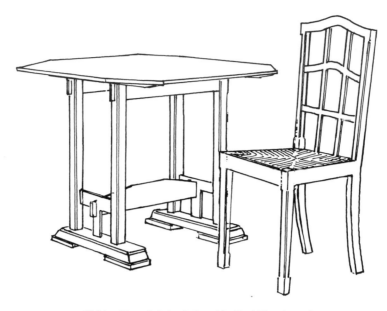

Welsh table and chair, designed by Paul Matt (*c*.1935)

During the Victorian craze for carving antique chests and coffers, many plain examples from Wales were sent to England to suffer this fate. Large numbers of dressers and settles were also imported into England and became very popular when the collecting of antique furniture gathered pace in the 1920s.

In the 1930s a successful furniture making business was established in Breconshire, employing many men, in the town of Brynmawr, where unemployment had been very high. With showrooms in London they produced well designed modern furniture of a high standard of craftsmanship. The Brynmawr and Clydach Valley Industries came to an end with the second world war. A table and chair in oak is shown here which was designed for the firm by Paul Matt about 1935 (see figure).

(See also the following entries, for examples of Welsh furniture: *Ark: Bed; Bench; Box; Chair; Chest; Cupboard; Dresser; Settle; Table*.)

Willow A light, soft, white wood which was stained black as a substitute for ebony in the 17th and 18th centuries.

Wych elm (*Ulmus glabra*) A native British tree giving a hard, pale, reddish brown wood used for chairmaking and sometimes for panelling. Also used by wheelwrights for the shafts of farm carts or other purposes requiring special strength.

X-chair An X-frame chair made by coffermakers; see *Cofferer*.

Yew (*Taxus baccata*) A native British tree giving a hard red-brown wood that takes a good polish. It is very resistant to wear and decay and was used for the turned work of Windsor chairs. Some of the best-made and best-designed Windsor chairs are made in yew, showing it was a wood favoured by the more skilled craftsmen.

The Care and Preservation of Wood

The best treatment for the care of solid wood furniture is the same today as it was in the 16th and 17th centuries, when the popularity of it was at its height, that is beeswax or linseed oil.

Probably the earliest furniture was left untreated or else painted. Traces of colour can still be seen on some of the earliest pieces. But from an early date beeswax was used as a protective finish, accounting for the gradual darkening of early oak, as the beeswax absorbed dirt and darkened the wood.

Home-made beeswax polish The polish can be made at home by slowly melting three parts of natural beeswax with nine parts of real turpentine *over a double saucepan*, or else in a *tin standing in a saucepan of hot water*. This is most important; the melting point of beeswax is $65\,^{\circ}\mathrm{C}$ ($149\,^{\circ}\mathrm{F}$) and it is dangerous to heat the mixture over a naked flame as the turpentine is very inflammable. Carnauba wax added to the mixture gives a harder finish to the wood. This will give a dark polish, and if a lighter polish is wanted bleached beeswax can be used.

Paraffin wax is cheaper and will also give a lighter colour if added, but the polish will not be so hard. It should be the consistency of a stiff paste when cold, and should be stored in a tightly lidded tin.

The polish should be applied with a soft cloth, lint free as the lint would stick to the wax, or with a brush to carvings and mouldings. The first application should be left for 24 hours before polishing and the process can be repeated until the desired finish is obtained.

Oil, and oil varnishes Oil was also used on early furniture and gives a good protective surface, especially on table tops, if used every few months with plenty of rubbing with a soft cloth in between. Only a little oil should be applied at a time. If too much oil – or wax – has built up on furniture over the years it can be removed with a little turpentine, and the surface well dried before more oil or wax is applied.

An alternative mixture for cleaning can be made from one part each of turpentine, linseed oil and vinegar and a quarter of a part of methylated spirit well shaken and applied sparingly with cotton wool. Soft clean cloths should always be used for the care of furniture, with plenty of hard rubbing. If a small amount of oil is applied daily for several weeks a really hardwearing surface will be produced. Once this surface has been obtained it can be maintained by only occasional rubbing with small amounts of oil.

Oil varnishes can be used and were used on oak and walnut furniture in the late 17th century, but care must be used in applying it. The surface must be very clean and dry, and the piece of furniture kept in a dry, clean, draught-free atmosphere between applications of the varnish; about three coats are needed to give a good finish. Once this is obtained simply rubbing with a soft cloth should be enough to keep the surface in good condition. A poor varnish finish can also be improved by a small application of linseed oil well rubbed in.

Avoiding shrinkage Probably most damage to antique furniture today is caused by central heating. Wood is a live material and swells and shrinks with changes in the atmosphere. When it is still growing the bark serves to protect it from excessive heat or cold or attacks by insects. But once it is turned into furniture conditions that are too hot or too dry cause shrinkage and consequent cracks, so furniture too near radiators or storage heaters will soon suffer unless a humidifier is used. A small dish of water in the room can provide the necessary rise in humidity. Damp conditions can also cause trouble; wood will swell when the atmosphere is too damp.

Woodworm Furniture should be constantly examined for signs of activity by woodworm, the larvae of the furniture beetle. Much old furniture has holes of previous attacks by woodworm, but if there is no sign of recent activity this does not matter. The woodworm are usually introduced into the home in a piece of furniture of wood or wickerwork already infected. The grub bores into the wood to obtain nourishment and shelter over a period of anything from one to five years. During this time the wood is being tunnelled and weakened. At the end of the feeding stage the grub excavates a cell just below the surface of the wood, where it changes into a pupa. When in a few weeks time the pupa becomes a beetle it bites through the thin film of wood to freedom leaving the tell-tale worm holes.

This happens between May to August. If during this period wood dust falls from the worm holes it is a sign that the woodworm in the furniture is active and it should be treated at once with a liquid insecticide especially for the treatment of woodworm. This will be successful in proportion to the penetration of the wood achieved by its application. Its object is to kill any grubs still in the woodwork, and to impregnate the wood with a persistent poison that will be fatal to any grubs infesting it in the future. The fluid must therefore be applied liberally to all absorbent surfaces, particularly the backs and bottom of case furniture and injected into all wormholes. Repeat process for two consecutive years at least.

Where to See Country Furniture

These are just some of the museums and houses open to the public where examples of furniture mentioned in the book can be seen:

American Museum in Britain, Claverton Manor, Bath, Somerset.
Angus Folk Collection, Glamis, Angus.
Aston Hall, Birmingham.
Breamore House, nr. Fordingbridge, Hampshire.
Bridewell Museum of Local Industries and Rural Crafts, Norwich, Norfolk.
Chambercombe Manor, Ilfracombe, Devon.
Christchurch Mansion, Ipswich, Suffolk.
Dorset Country Museum, Dorchester, Dorset.
Gladstone Court, Biggar, Lanarkshire.
Great Chalfield Manor, Melksham, Wiltshire.
Highland Folk Museum, Kingussie, Inverness, Scotland.
High Wycombe Chair Museum, High Wycombe, Buckinghamshire.
Littlecote, nr. Hungerford, Wiltshire.
Museum of English Rural Life, Whiteknights Park, Reading, Berkshire.
National Museum of Antiquities of Scotland, Edinburgh.
North Cornwall Museum, Camelford, Cornwall.
Strangers' Hall, Norwich, Norfolk.
Tankerness House, Kirkwall, Orkney.
Temple Newsam House, Leeds.
Townend, Troutbeck, Cumbria.
Trerice, St. Newlyn East, Cornwall.
Welsh Folk Museum, St. Fagans, Glamorgan.
West Yorkshire Folk Museum, Shibden Hall, Halifax, Yorkshire.

Other museums and houses, together with opening times of the above can be found in the following publications which are published annually:

Historic Houses, Castles and Gardens in Great Britain and Ireland (ABC Travel Guides)
Museums and Galleries in Great Britain and Ireland (ABC Travel Guides)
Britain's Heritage (Automobile Association)

How to Find
Modern Craftsmen

A comprehensive guide to the whereabouts of contemporary country furniture makers is clearly beyond our scope, if only because today's craftsmen, like their forbears, tend to be highly individualistic and widely dispersed. But for anyone who wants to know more about the crafted furniture that is being produced today and who is drawn to visiting workshops where good furniture is being made with a view to buying or perhaps commissioning an individual piece, a brief note on some directions to follow may be helpful.

The chief source of information in this context is the CRAFTS ADVISORY COMMITTEE, an independent body whose aim is to promote Britain's artist craftsmen and to make known to the public where the work of craftsmen specializing in every branch of craft is to be seen and purchased. The address of the CAC is 12 Waterloo Place, London SW1 4AU (01-839 1917).

Among the CAC's many activities is an Index of Craftsmen, an illustrated guide to the work of a selected number of contemporary British craftsmen. The Index, consisting of colour slides and accompanying information, can be viewed without charge, by appointment, between 10 am to 5 pm Monday to Friday at the Waterloo Place Gallery, also at 12 Waterloo Place, where exhibitions of craft work are held regularly and where a wide range of specialized publications may be obtained. The Index shows not only what can be purchased but gives information about work that can be specially commissioned. A leaflet entitled *Index of Craftsmen: Furniture* is obtainable from the same address—one of a wide range of CAC publications which makes it well worth your while to visit their offices – or alternatively, if you are interested in other crafts besides furniture, *Craftsmen of Quality*, the illustrated guide to the Index, listing the full complement of craftsmen and costing £1.50 would be a good investment.

Apart from the Index, there is also a non-selective Register of craftsmen in England and Wales, arranged geographically, which may also be consulted by the public.

THE COUNCIL FOR SMALL INDUSTRIES IN RURAL AREAS (COSIRA) publish a useful handbook entitled *Craft Workshops in the Countryside*, which consists of a selected list of country craftsmen, county by county and craft by craft, throughout England and Wales, who are 'at home' to visitors wishing to see their workshops and buy their work. This contains detailed information about the speciality of each of the craftsmen listed and gives their addresses and 'opening hours'. It also indicates those craftsmen who are in the market for specially commissioned work. The handbook costs 75p (plus 20p postage) and is obtainable from COSIRA, Queen's House, Fish Row, Salisbury, Wiltshire, SP1 1EX.

Some guidelines on commissioning

If you decide you would like to have a piece of country furniture specially made for you, the first thing to do is to find a craftsman whose personal style is in keeping with your own tastes and needs. Although a craftsman will be willing to be adaptable to please his patron, he also needs a measure of 'elbow room' to do his best work – and if you have chosen the right person for what you want in the first place the chances of your both being happy with the result are obviously greater. So it is wise to see as much of his work as possible before asking him to make something for you. Unless you are absolutely certain of your choice, it's a good idea to draw up a short list of 'possibles' and go and see several craftsmen before deciding.

First, be clear in your own mind how much you are prepared to spend and what you want the object to 'do' for you. At the preliminary encounter, for which there is no charge, you will need to discuss the purpose of the object, the materials to be used and, of course, the fee.

If the commission is an uncomplicated one, you may be able to agree on the spot so that he can go ahead. For something more complex however, he will need to know how much you can afford and to prepare designs for you to approve; a fee will be payable for these which will have been agreed at the first meeting. After seeing the designs, if you are not satisfied that you will get what you want, you can withdraw without further obligation.

If you decide to go ahead you may then be asked to pay – on top of the design fee – a proportion of the total cost. He may also ask that the rest of the payment should be made in instalments as he goes along. Remember, if there is something you are not happy about, be sure to say so promptly rather than putting it off until the work has progressed too far for it to be altered.

As soon as the work is finished, it's only fair to settle the craftsman's bill promptly; keeping him waiting for his money might cause hardship and could certainly lead to bad feeling – which would spoil the pleasure of what should be a very rewarding and pleasurable relationship.

Bibliography

AGIUS, PAULINE: 'English Chairmakers listed in general and trade directories 1790–1851.' Furniture History Vol. XII 1976. (The Journal of the Furniture History Society)

ARONSON, JOSEPH: *Encyclopedia of Furniture* (Batsford) 1966.

BECK, DOREEN: *Book of American Furniture* (Hamlyn) 1973.

BIRD, ANTHONY: *English Furniture for the Private Collector* (Batsford) 1961.

BRANDER, MICHAEL: *Scottish Crafts and Craftsmen* (Johnston and Bacon) 1974.

BROWN, H. MILES: *Cornish Clocks and Clockmakers* (David and Charles) 1970.

CHINNERY, VICTOR: *The English Oak Tradition* (Antique Collectors' Club, Woodbridge, Suffolk) 1977.

GLOAG, JOHN: *English Furniture* (Adam and Charles Black) 1973.
A Short Dictionary of Furniture (Allen and Unwin) new edition 1976.
The Englishman's Chair (Allen and Unwin) 1964.

GRANT, I. F.: *Highland and Folk Ways* (Routledge and Kegan Paul) 1961.

HARRISON, JOHN: *A History of English Furniture* (Mills and Boon) 1972.

HAYDEN, ARTHUR: *Chats on Cottage and Farmhouse Furniture* (Unwin) 1912. (Revised Cyril Bunt, Ernest Benn 1950).

HAYWARD, CHARLES: *English Period Furniture* (Evans Bros) 1971.

JEKYLL, GERTRUDE: *Old West Surrey* (Longmans Green) 1904.

JEKYLL, GERTRUDE: *Old English Household Life* (Batsford) 1975.

JENKINS, A. K. HAMILTON: *Cornwall and its People* (David and Charles) 1970.

JENKINS, J. GERAINT: *Traditional Country Craftsmen* (Routledge and Kegan Paul) 1965.

JOY, EDWARD T.: *Antique English Furniture* (Ward Lock) 1972.
The Country Life Book of English Furniture 1964.
Furniture (The Connoisseur) 1972.

LAYCOCK, CHARLES H.: *The Old Devon Farmhouse*: Report and Transactions of the Devonshire Association. Vol. LIV 1923. Vol. LV. 1924.

LOUDON, J. C.: *Encyclopedia of Cottage, Farm and Villa Architecture and Furniture* (1833).
Loudon's Furniture Designs. (E. P. Publishing, Wakefield, Yorkshire).

OLIVE, GABRIEL: 'Furniture in a West Country Parish 1576–1769'.
'"American" Windsor Chairs from Devon'.
Furniture History. Vol. XII 1976.

ORMSBEE, THOMAS H.: *The Windsor Chair.* (Allen) 1962.

REEVES, DAVID: *Furniture – An Explanatory History* (Faber) 1959.

ROE, F. GORDON: *English Cottage Furniture* (Phoenix) 1961.
Victorian Furniture (Phoenix) 1952.
Windsor Chairs (Phoenix) 1953.

ROGERS, JOHN C.: *English Furniture* (Country Life) 1959.

ROSE, WALTER: *The Village Carpenter* (E.P. Publishing, Wakefield, Yorkshire) 1973.

SHEA, JOHN G.: *Antique Country Furniture of North America* (Evans Bros) 1976.

SPARKES, IVAN G.: *The English Country Chair* (Spurbooks Ltd) 1973.
  The Windsor Chair (Spurbooks Ltd) 1975.

STEER, FRANCIS W. *Farm and Cottage Inventories of Mid-Essex 1635–1749* (Phillimore and Co. Ltd, Chichester) 1969.

TWISTON-DAVIES, L. and H. J. LLOYD-JOHNES.: *Welsh Furniture* (University of Wales Press) 1950.

TEMPLE NEWSAM HOUSE, Leeds: *Oak Furniture from Gloucestershire and Somerset.* Catalogue 1976.

TOLLER, JANE: *Country Furniture* (David and Charles) 1973.

VICTORIA AND ALBERT MUSEUM: *English Chairs*. 1965.

WELLS-COLE, ANTHONY: *Oak Furniture in Dorset*. Furniture History Vol XII. 1976.

WOLSEY, S. W. and R. W. P. LUFF: *Furniture in England: The Age of the Joiner* (Arthur Barker) 1968.

Index

Bold numerals indicate a main entry; those in italics indicate an illustration

Dictionary of Country Furniture

The sturdy simplicity and mellowed warmth of old country furniture is perfectly in tune with the 'back-to-essentials' feel of the mid-seventies. For anyone who is drawn to collecting the well-made, humbler furniture of our ancestors, *Dictionary of Country Furniture* is the ideal book. It is both a practical, lavishly illustrated guide which will help the reader to identify a particular piece seen in a sale room or antique shop, and a handbook providing the historical framework to which to relate it.

Covering unsophisticated pieces made in the rural areas of England, Wales and Scotland mainly in the eighteenth century through to modern times, the book includes a number of items – from dower chests to Windsor chairs – that are of particular interest to the North American reader.

Alphabetically arranged for easy reference, the main part includes both individual items of furniture, definitions of technical terms, the characteristics of regional groups and the function of the various craftsmen. The historical factors which have influenced the development of country furniture are outlined in the introduction, and the final section lists museums and other places where fine specimens can be seen.

Marjorie Filbee has written extensively on archaeology and on many aspects of country life for a number of magazines and periodicals. Throughout her studies the connecting thread has been her interest in the history of the homes of country people.